FOURTEEN DAYS OF EATING IN A REAL FOOD WAY!

"Just keep it real, honey!"

BY

CHEF SHANE KELLY

Cover Photograph taken at Delvin Farms, College Grove, TN by Mike Rapp

Back cover photograph by Juan Pont Lezica

TABLE OF CONTENTS

FOREWORD

"The aim of medicine is to prevent disease and prolong life; the ideal of medicine is to eliminate the need of a physician."

William J Mayo (1861-1939 A.D.)

Isn't it a glorious miracle that healing happens? We really do not consider this everyday marvel very often. The body and mind are constantly recovering and adapting to cope with challenges of gravity, toxicity, friction, rusting, erosion, time and space. When you cut a steak it does not heal – but when you cut your arm it knits itself back into a form that can again function. This remarkable capacity is the process of Health Creation, and leveraging the ability of the body to do this more effectively has been my life's passion.

Again and again in the realm of prevention and treatment of chronic illness we come to find that the gut is at the center of much of our troubles and our opportunity. Within the gut we find the vast majority of our immune system - which is the engine for the creation of inflammation – which is increasingly getting the attention it deserves as a major cause of degenerative illnesses of all types. From Alzheimer's, to coronary heart disease, to diabetes, to Parkinson's, to Depression, to auto-immune illness, to macular degeneration, etc., the gut plays an important contributory role. So what we put in that gut matters on the most profound of levels.

The types and quality of food we choose to consume on a daily basis is the foundation of health creation. Each of us individually choosing to consume higher quality foods with greater consistency is a far more important and influential "Health Reform" than ever we could see from Washington D.C.

Not only do our foods fuel our day to day activity, they also provide the raw-materials to make our cells, hormones, and neurotransmitters. Our food may most accurately be understood as information which our cells 'listen to' and change in accordance with the message being sent. Trans-fats and fructose send messages of alarm to the cells which turn on genes that promote inflammation and insulin resistance. Conversely healthy omega-3 fats turn on families of genes that turn off inflammation, and compounds in broccoli seeds turn on genes to improve cellular detoxification.

I use these compounds in concentrated forms in my practice of nutritional medicine – and I tell all my patients that supplements, no matter how helpful, are supplemental to a high-quality whole foods diet. The question often arises, "What is that and where do I start?" Part of the answer is sitting in your hands. Chef Shane Kelly has done a wonderful job of bringing out the best of the taste and balance of whole foods within this book.

Do yourself a favor. Invest the time, attention and energy to engage this process for 14 days. You may find you feel remarkably better – and even if the changes are not as profound as you had hoped, you will be well along the road to preventing the suffering of disability and the tragedy of premature aging and death.   Whole foods heal.

Thanks Chef Shane Kelly!

David H. Haase, MD
Founder, MaxWell Clinic for Proactive Medicine
CMO, the LifeStrive Group
Clarksville, TN

INTRODUCTION

Eat outside the box! Because in most cases, eating the box would probably be better for you!

Well, it's no secret that eating out of boxes has gotten us into a lot of trouble over the last 60 or more years. When I think about how many modern-day illnesses there are, one big question I ask is, "what have we been eating?" Although there's no doubt that toxins in our environment have done a lot to wreak havoc on our health as well. But, in my opinion it is <u>what</u> we've been consuming that is at the core of these modern-day diseases and the increased frequency of older diseases that we have had to endure. Think about the way our ancestors ate more than one hundred years ago. Theirs was a diet of lard, whole full-fat raw milk/dairy, butter, eggs, meat cooked on the bone with the fat, well you get the idea. Most people are horrified by the aforementioned foods today because we've been brainwashed into believing that, among other things, "all fat is bad." Way back then, heart disease was rare, type II diabetes was rare and obesity for sure, was rare. In most cases, the folks who contracted those diseases ate a lot of refined sugar and flour. I know we're also not nearly as active as they were back then but, the biggest difference is in what we eat today compared to what they ate then; nutrient-dense foods. I'm not talking about the synthetic vitamins and minerals they add into manufactured foods and drinks today because the nutrients were all destroyed during processing of the foods, I'm talking about eating foods that have all of their nutrients intact to begin with -- whole food! In order to have optimal health and to be firing on all cylinders, your body needs to be fed ALL the goodness of real food!

I was inspired to write this "eating plan" if you will, because every time I gave a speech on why it's important to eat "real food" members of the audience asked if I would consider writing down all this information? So, this eating guide is my talk about nutrient-dense foods put into a very practical every day application of what to eat for breakfast, lunch, dinner and snacks. We are so bombarded with information every day about what's good for us and what isn't and a lot of this information can contradict itself. With "14 Days of Eating in a Real Food Way!" I hope to help you demystify and simplify a real, nutrient-dense way of eating.

"Eat outside the box" means two things to me:
1. Break free of "food numbers" like grams and calories and eat real foods that don't have any numbers written on them.
2. And literally, eat out of as few boxes as you possibly can.

If you do these two things then you'll be way ahead of the game! Just remember that, 80-90% of all disease and illness is preventable through diet and exercise with a much heavier emphasis on the importance of what you eat. If that statistic doesn't inspire you I don't know what will. Wow, to think that for the majority of the time I actually have something to say about the status of my health! Think of it this way, with every bite of food you take you are either supporting your health or tearing it down, it's that simple. So let my "14 Days of Eating in a Real Food Way!" help you make better choices!

FOOD SHOULD EQUATE TO YOUR SATISFACTION, HEALTH AND WELL BEING!

First of all, food should taste good, right? For instance, I don't know many people who really enjoy fat-free anything – well maybe if you liked eating paste as a kid – but if you did, you might want to keep that little fact to yourself. If you don't eat food that tastes good & is satisfying, then your body will tell you, "There was something NOT quite right about what you fed me because I'm still hungry." You should feel good, nourished, calm and satisfied after you eat. If your body isn't being fed satisfying, nutrient-dense foods then you will stay hungry and keep craving and eating foods that don't support your health. This is the vicious cycle most of us experience and the main reason why obesity is at such epic proportions right now. "Fat-free" is dead wrong.

When I say "nutrient-dense" foods, I mean foods with all of their vitamins and minerals intact. Consider this: our bodies are highly intelligent and they know they need nutrients, vitamins and minerals from food to function at the most basic level; when your body realizes it's not getting the nutrition it needs to survive it just keeps craving food...so we keep eating more wrong stuff, still not satisfying our bodies, and hence, the weight gain. Eating "nutrient-vacant foods" will make you sick one way or the other and there is no

©2010 Chef Shane Kelly, LLC   - 9 -

way around that one. Again, real food is your ticket to satisfaction, health and well being!

I guess by now you can really tell that I'm super passionate about people eating real, whole food because I know the difference it can make first hand! So, this is my life work now – my calling. In 2005 I graduated from "The Natural Gourmet Institute for Health and Culinary Arts" in New York City and feel so well-equipped to talk to you about real food nutrition because of that amazing school and all the other reading/cooking/researching I've done on my own. I now teach real food cooking classes and talk to groups about how to "just keep it real, honey!" What's most thrilling to me is when people start to make better choices in their diet and as a result notice how much better they feel, and how much better their kids behave.

A lot of what I will say to you in this booklet will go against "conventional wisdom" and make you pause and say, "are you kidding me?" All I'm asking is that you resist this conventional wisdom and try some of the changes I am suggesting for a few weeks and then see how you feel. So hang with me and give it a try.

Just so you know, (and for legal reasons) I need to remind everyone that I am not a doctor, nutritionist, dietitian, magician or your mama! And, if you take my advice you might just get into better health, imagine that! But, if you don't feel better with what I'm recommending then stop doing it and go back to eating in your box-crazed way. Keep in mind though that you will need to "detox" from boxed-food eating and retrain your taste buds on what real food and real-food nutrition tastes like.

Just consider that my eating plan is my commentary about good food and food that is good for you! It is important to note that I am not recommending these dietary changes for people whose health is compromised. Of course whole foods are good for you but you may have a condition where what I'm recommending won't work for you, so I suggest you consult your physician first. As a matter of fact, I recommend that everyone consult their physician first before embarking on a new way of eating.

Whew, now that I've gotten that out of the way...

Learning how to eat in a health-supportive way is a process. Let me repeat this...you will not change the way you eat overnight and stick with it, so take it a step at a time. It's taken me about 9 years to get to where I am and yet, I still find things in my pantry that I have to throw out because I finally decided to read the label. Maybe one week you'll focus on only eating unrefined sweeteners and the next week you'll only eat "whole" grains or take longer getting adjusted to a certain step if you need to.

Please know that I've definitely been known to sit down to a sub-zero "health-supportive" food item and really enjoy it, knowing that I will feel like crud later, but I had fun while it lasted. Sometimes you just have to go there. And by all means don't become a "food zealot" at least not in public, because we want to inspire people to make better food choices and not be annoyed by people who want to eat real food.

There's a happy medium in all of this and you'll find yours. Relax, be thoughtful about your food, where and how was it grown and be sure to give thanks for the hands that prepared it. Make good food choices -- then eat it and enjoy it!

Finally, one other note about feeling good and how intelligent our bodies are. Think of all the systems in our bodies as self-regulating. Kinda like the way your thermostat keeps your house temperature regulated. If you become a "real foodie," but are overriding many of your other self-regulating mechanisms, you will still feel bad. This is where it helps to keep an eye on sleep, exercise, drinking plenty of water, keeping stress levels in check, emotion, faith, etc. You can have a fast car, with great fuel (real food) but just try and go fast with just three wheels! Our bodies are miraculous, highly integrated systems that have in many cases been pushed way beyond "normal operating limits." (Much more on that to come...)

RULES OF THE ROAD FOR YOUR REAL FOOD JOURNEY!

This two week plan focuses on late spring and summer foods. I love eating fresh and in-season foods because the taste is far better than what I can find in most grocery stores where the produce was harvested "weeks" before in a very far away place...in most cases. Thankfully, more and more grocery stores are starting to carry produce from local farmers so kudos to them! I believe the most nourishing and tastiest food is the freshest food and what better time for real food abundance than summer? So enjoy the season of bounty and buy locally grown foods as much as you are able! Taste and feel the difference!

Parts of the Plan:

Eating Guide:
You will find 2 full weeks of suggested meals for breakfast, lunch, dinner and snacks, in which I hope to show you what a balanced meal and snack might look like. It's always important when eating a meal or a snack to have a healthy balance of good fat, protein and carbohydrate...without having to count calories and grams. I also built in meals using leftovers which I know makes a lot of busy folks happy, me included!

Shopping List:
Each week will have its own shopping list that you can take to the farmer's market and grocery store to tell you what you need to have on hand for the week to make the suggested recipes. Be sure to check the list

first before shopping to make sure you don't already have some of the items in your kitchen.

Recipes:
Anywhere that I have recommended a specific dish there will be a page number next to it to get you to the recipe quickly in the back of this booklet. And, if I've recommended an uncommon food ingredient then I will go into some explanation about it at the end of the recipe and where you can find it. I also want to mention that the majority of my recipes are gluten-free and can be changed to gluten-free if they are not already so.

Sweets and sweet food:
It's true we all have a sweet tooth but in America we've moved way beyond a sweet tooth to a "sweet body" and it's tearing our health down as a nation...no one can dispute that. I'm not a huge fan of sweet food because I believe if we eat a lot of sweets or foods that raise our blood sugar levels then we crash and crave something sweet all over again to lift us back up and so the vicious cycle of craving and crashing continues. So, when I offer a "sweet" dish you will notice that it is very low in "sugar" in most, most cases. So your palette may have to adjust a bit to something being less sweet. But, keep in mind, the more nutrient-dense foods you consume with enough good healthy fats, the less likely you are to crave any sweets. But, I do add in a little honey, maple syrup and sucanat (organic evaporated cane juice) to recipes here and there...but, not enough to throw you out of balance. If you do find yourself craving sweets then eat a piece of real cheese or a big spoonful of

nut butter, drink some water, breathe and it should pass.

This is a very manageable eating plan because I only have you making about three new recipes a day because I didn't want you to be overwhelmed by making a lot of new food every day. Just enjoy making several things and let them sink in and try something new. Take it slow but, stick with it.

I kept lunches very simple and essentially just a recommendation. I tried to keep all the recipes kid-friendly but keep in mind if you like things spicier and don't have little ones eating with you then knock yourself out and throw in the "hot stuff." Most kids seemed to enjoy the recipes once they got past the tasting phase so, don't give up. Keep getting your kids to try new things and more than once if you can. I find that as long as food tastes good, has a good amount of "good" fat on/in it and is well seasoned then kids will at least try it and will probably like it.

Speaking of the recipes I want to give a special shout out and thank you to my "recipe testing Mama's" who were so committed to trying this more nutrient-dense way of eating to nourish themselves and their families. Special thanks to Susan, Melisa, Courtney, Jennifer, Jennifer, Gina, Hannah and Cady...you gals are awesome and I so appreciate your help!

My Philosophy on Fats

In the past when I've eaten a diet very low in fat and "bad" fats at that, I have felt awful – unsatisfied after a meal or snack, anxious, sometimes depressed, gotten sick more often, become heavier in my mid-section, had a hard time focusing, not slept all that well, and I'll just stop there. I love to be a guinea pig and eat all types of things just to see how it affects me and then I can share my findings with you. So that's what I did by eating lots of nutrient-dense fats and I haven't tried any other fats since. You're wondering, "What kind of fats are you talking about?" Here's what I do and don't recommend incorporating into your diet: real butter (cream, maybe a culture, salt...these should be the only ingredients that you see in your butter), absolutely NO "spreads" or butter substitutes of any kind, ever; whole fat dairy (organic is preferable); virgin (unrefined) coconut oil; extra-virgin olive oil; bacon fat rendered from nitrate/nitrite-free bacon, ghee (butter with all the milk solids removed, great for higher-heat cooking), unrefined flax seed oil (never cook with this); expeller-pressed nut and seed oils which, for the most part should not be heated and should be used very sparingly; occasionally you can cook with unrefined peanut oil to fry and sesame oil for a stir-fry because they are fairly stable at high temperatures and have antioxidant benefits but are fairly high in omega-6 which is why they should only be used occasionally. Then, when you become a true fat-convert you will start eating some lard from a local farmer (not the hydrogenated stuff that's in the grocery store) and duck/goose fat...see what you have to look forward to? ☺

Keep in mind we were eating a lot of those fats mentioned above long before we introduced all these rancid, processed vegetable and seed oils to our food supply which have created such inflammation and oxidation in our bodies. And when we were eating all those good, real, nutrient-dense fats giving us all those great fat-soluble vitamins A, K, D & E...heart disease and diabetes were very, very rare. The first trans-fat, (we'll just call it "shortening") was invented in 1911. So, you do the math and take a guess as to one of the biggest reasons why the health of this country started failing so many years ago and is still headed south.

A lot of what I know about real good fat and other foods comes from the "Weston A. Price Foundation" www.westonaprice.org. Please take the time to visit their website for the science on the goodness of real fats...you will be amazed. Sally Fallon Morell, president of the Weston A. Price Foundation and Mary G. Enig, Ph.D. (world expert on lipids/fats) are doing a remarkable job of getting the good news out about eating lots of real, nutrient-dense foods in their books: "Nourishing Traditions" by Sally Fallon Morell with Mary G. Enig, Ph.D. and "Eat Fat, Lose Fat" by Morell and Enig, which focuses mostly on the huge benefits of incorporating unrefined coconut oil into our everyday diets.

Why Soak Grains?

In some recipes you'll read that I want you to soak oatmeal in water and a little lemon juice or buttermilk depending on what you're making and brown rice and water with a little lemon juice as well. Traditional cultures would have never dreamed of harvesting a grain and just eating it. They knew instinctively that they were just too hard to digest. When you soak a grain in water and a little acid (lemon juice, apple cider vinegar, whey) it begins to break the grain down (pre-digesting it) therefore making it easier for our body to digest so that we'll be able to assimilate more of the nutrients that the grain has to offer. Plus, the grain cooks a lot faster, is creamier and more important, it's tastier too!

Read the Recipe Please

The reason I want to draw attention to this is that I have had some folks and I'm guilty of this too, rush through reading the recipe once and then begin making it and invariably, steps get skipped and frustration ensues. So let me recommend that you read each recipe through 2-3 times in its entirety and you'll be good to go. Prep all your ingredients before you begin the cooking process because it creates a more pleasant experience once you begin cooking. And, please read any food notes that I have written around a recipe because it's going to give you more information about an ingredient or cooking technique that may help you in the making of that recipe.

Cooking Through One Week

Most of the folks who recipe tested this two-week period for me said that they just took their time and it took about 2 weeks to work through one week. That's great, because by taking your time and hopefully starting to incorporate foods that you haven't eaten on a regular basis before, you'll be more inclined to stick with the changes you're making. As you know, <u>this is not a diet, but a way of eating and supporting the health of you and your family</u>!

Local Farmers and a Fair Price for Their Food

If you spend any time on my website you'll see that I have a great love for the local farmer. When you think about how hard they work to nourish their family and community and barely make a living doing it...it just makes me very grateful. This is why we need to work hard to adjust our thinking that "food should be cheap." That's a long and tragic story about how we got to the state of "cheap food" and we'll save it for another time. The production of real, nutrient-dense foods should not be cheap because it is labor intensive...and why do you want to put cheap food into your temple all the time anyway? My Mama, May Fair, always told me that she hoped that I would always budget for good quality food. Keep in mind, you can either "pay now or pay later" and that's the hard truth. So try to look at the true cost of food and start to invest in your local farmer who will support your health if you help them...what a rewarding and beautiful relationship that is! So find and visit your local farmer's market on a regular basis and you'll be so happy you did...even if you just start by buying a dozen eggs!

So let's just leave it here with the local farmer. Eat fresh, real, and local as much as possible and you will feel the difference and love the results!

Please don't hesitate to contact me at: shane@chefshanekelly.com with any questions or ideas you may have to share about your experience of eating in a real food way. I want to hear from you!

My Wake-Up Call!

If you've read the Introduction of this book you're probably asking yourself, "Why is this woman so passionate about people focusing on eating whole, nutrient-dense foods?" Well, as they say, everyone has a story, and here's mine, relative to food and healing.

In the years leading up to our late 30's most of our bodies can endure all kinds of abuse in the form of bad food, too much alcohol, lack of sleep, stress, and other unsavory things. It has been my experience that the human body is very forgiving. But, like all things in life, our bodies have a breaking point, too. Make no mistake about it, if you're paying attention you will know when that breaking point begins.

At about age 40 I was getting all sorts of "warning signs." I was 25-30 pounds overweight, I had terrible acid reflux, poor digestion, really painful PMS/periods, constipation, poor sleep patterns, bloated belly, heart palpitations, low energy and some depression thrown in for good measure. So, needless to say, I wasn't exactly the life of the party at this point in my life. Along with all these physical challenges I took the corresponding over-the-counter drugs to ease my "symptoms." Notice, the light bulb hadn't gone off yet telling me, "Maybe you need to change the way you're eating and see if that doesn't alleviate any of these problems."

So, I kept living with these "challenges" until I got the big wake-up call. Mind you, every last one of those things on my list in the previous paragraph was a wake-up call, but obviously not enough to get my attention. It was time for my annual gynecological exam and for the first time in my life I received an irregular pap smear report. Well, you can bet the red lights started flashing for me then. I knew deep down that what I was eating and drinking had a lot to do with my poor health, but it took this fateful visit to the Gyno to finally wake me up! I am still thankful for this wake-up call. I told the doctor to give me about three months and I would be back for a follow-up pap smear to see if things had gotten worse or better.

Instead of me boring you with all my research regarding my "old" condition, I will just tell you that it became clear to me that I needed to "clean house." The word cleanse conjures up all kinds of bad images for a lot of people as it did for me but I took the relatively easy cleanse road and have never looked back. I had been having digestive issues for a long time and now it was time to control the situation. As Hippocrates said, "All disease begins in the gut." So it was time for me to clean up my gut.

For about two months I ate nothing but a little oatmeal, brown rice, extra-virgin olive oil, ghee (clarified butter with no milk solids), lean protein of fish and chicken, all vegetables, mostly green ones though, lemon, water, herbal tea, etc. I did not consume any dairy or wheat/gluten because they are quite difficult to digest for most people. You get the idea though, very clean eating and drinking. I will tell you right up front it was hard at first and you feel like you have the flu for a week or two depending on what kind of shape you are in going into the cleanse. But, coming out of it I felt like new money and wasn't taking any more over-the-counter anything. Yea!!! It was kind of like the feeling you get when you become debt free. Well, free!

Now that I was taking steps to support my health like: eating nothing but whole, mostly organic locally grown foods, drinking lots of good filtered water, sleeping, eliminating regularly (sorry, that's not very romantic, but critical), exercising and taking supplements that were specific to my specific needs. I then set the appointment to see my gynecologist for the follow-up pap smear exam. A few days later she let me know that all was well and I had a clean bill of health and have ever since, thank the good Lord!

I wanted to tell you this story because I know first-hand how to help heal yourself with food. I see so many people physically challenged in ways that aren't necessary. Since our bodies are so forgiving it really doesn't take a huge effort to feel better. Please just consider that good health, in most cases, is your birthright. God gives us that gift right off the bat. Isn't that great news?!

I have a wonderful mother, May Fair who fed me lots of "good food" when I was under her roof. I always remember eating balanced and delicious meals from Mama's kitchen. We didn't have candy, sodas and lots of snacky foods lying around the house and for this I am so grateful to her. Even though I ate pretty well after leaving home I started to eat more and more processed convenience foods because I was so "busy." And so the vicious cycle began. Eat bad food, feel bad, take meds to deal with bad symptoms, feel worse, eat bad food for comfort and so it goes until I broke the cycle and took control of my own health.

I'm grateful that I went through all that I did with my health because that is when I heard the calling to switch careers and become a "whole food preacher!" I was also given the gift of the wake-up call so that I could speak to you about how to heal or just feel good by eating whole, nutrient-dense foods.

If I inspire you to make one positive change in your way of eating then I will have succeeded. Because I know once you take that first great step to "Just keep it real, honey!" you will feel the difference and take another step because it will get − oh so good! − to you. Everything will feel lighter and you'll feel more confident in all you do because you'll be nourished. You'll love better, focus better, work better, parent better, pray better, serve better because all that you'll be doing by eating wonderful real food will enhance your satisfaction, health and well-being!

"We are indeed much more than what we eat, but what we eat can nevertheless help us to be much more than what we are."

Adelle Davis

"14 Days of Eating in a Real Food Way"

WEEK ONE

DAY 1

BREAKFAST
*Note to self: Don't forget to soak your oatmeal the night before...just refer to the attached recipe.
Quick-Cooking Real Oatmeal (Page 52)
And all the fixin's!

LUNCH
Sandwich with whole-grain bread
*I recommend Ezekiel or Alvarado St. Bakery because they have the least "tragic" ingredients. Both of these breads and others can be found in most grocery stores in the frozen "health food" bread section. Toasting this bread makes it taste a whole lot better. Sourdough whole-grain bread is another good option.
*Buy deli meats with no nitrates or nitrites (these are preservatives and believed to cause cancer...so why chance it?). Or you can just make your own deli meat such as, chicken and turkey breast and then you know what you're getting.

*Some recommended deli meats:
Wellshire Farm Products
Applegate Farms
Hormel Natural Choice
Boar's Head Natural (be specific asking for these at the deli counter)

Salad with homemade dressings:
Ranch Dressing (Page 133)
Honey Balsamic Vinaigrette (Page 134)

*Do yourself a favor and make a big salad early in the week that you can eat on for the next 3 days and make enough dressing for the entire week. To keep the salad fresh, spread a damp paper towel over the top of the salad and seal the bowl with plastic wrap.

SNACK
Roasted Red Pepper Hummus (Page 121)
Carrot, celery sticks and whole-grain crackers

DINNER
Salmon with Lemon-Dill Butter (Page 113)
Creamed Spinach (Page 71)
Roasted Asparagus (Page 73)
Quinoa – Just follow the directions on the box. Be sure to wash the Quinoa well in a hand strainer, shake off all the water, proceed with the package cooking directions. Double the recipe since you'll be eating it for lunch one day and using a heaping cup of cooked Quinoa in your meatloaf recipe later in the week. Quinoa can be found in most grocery stores and certainly in your local health-food store. Just buy the plain-brown Quinoa. This is a very nutritious grain/seed that is high in protein and so easy to cook!

DAY 2

BREAKFAST
Easy-Bake Sausage or Bacon (Page 54)
Be sure to save bacon drippings for other cooking uses. Just store the bacon drippings in a little glass jar in the fridge.
Note: Buy bacon and sausage with no nitrites/nitrates.
Whole-grain cheese toast or with butter and all-fruit jam
A little side of fruit if you're so inclined.

LUNCH
Chef salad with the meat or cheese of your choice along with a small handful of walnuts and olives. Note: Please eat only "real" cheese and nothing processed.
Honey-Balsamic Vinaigrette (Page 134)
Ranch Dressing (Page 133)
Whole-grain crackers

SNACK
Granola Bars (Page 123)

DINNER
Spicy-Roasted Chicken and Sweet Potatoes (Page 101)
Broth-Steamed Broccoli (Page 74)

DAY 3

BREAKFAST
Egg and Must-Go Veggie Pie (Page 55)
This is so easy to make and delicious! Use the leftover creamed spinach and asparagus or some other favorite veggies from the week.
Toast with butter and real fruit jam

LUNCH
Leftover Quinoa
Canned wild salmon with lemon juice or Chipotle Tobasco Sauce
*This hot sauce is delicious and so flavorful and not that hot. You should be able to find it wherever they sell Tobasco Sauce. You'll also be using this in the "Herbed Meatloaf" recipe as well.
Leftover -- Broth-Steamed Broccoli (Page 74)

SNACK
Banana with nut butter

DINNER
Tomato Basil Soup with Coconut Milk (Page 137)
Roasted Chicken and Cheese Quesadillas (Page 103)
Tortillas should be whole-grain or 100% corn tortillas
*You can use leftover chicken from Monday night...or a rotisserie chicken from the store, just make sure you shred it.
A little side salad with homemade dressing

DAY 4

BREAKFAST
Organic whole-fat plain yogurt with cinnamon, a bit of maple syrup, fruit and ground flax seed
One slice of whole grain bread and a "smear" of nut butter

LUNCH
Salad with feta cheese and deli meats, sunflower seeds and homemade dressing.
Whole-grain crackers

SNACK
Roasted red pepper hummus (Page 121)
Vegetables for dipping

DINNER
Herbed Meatloaf (Page 105)
Oven-Roasted Yukon Gold Potatoes (Page 76)
Sweet Red Onion Green Beans (Page 78)

**While you're putting together dinner go ahead and wash and soak the brown rice that you'll be cooking tomorrow night. See the recipe and directions for this on page 131.

Little side of sauerkraut...just try it! Only buy the kind that has these three ingredients: water, cabbage and salt. That's it. It's fermented so it helps you digest the protein/meatloaf in your meal and enhances the bioavailability of the nutrients in all the food you eat. And, because true sauerkraut is made through a lacto-fermentation process your intestines will benefit from all the "good" bacteria it offers, too. It is a very health-supportive food!

DAY 5

BREAKFAST
Leftover – Egg and Must-Go Veggie Pie (Page 55)
Whole-grain bread with butter and fruit jam

LUNCH
Whole-grain bread sandwich with lettuce, tomato and leftover chicken (chopped and mixed with a little mayo and mustard to moisten)
Apple

SNACK
Granola Bar, crumbled into ½ cup of full-fat plain yogurt sweetened with a little pure maple syrup (I'm talking one teaspoon) and a little real fruit.

DINNER
Chicken Sausage and Peppers (Page 107)
Brown Rice (Page 131)
Zucchini, Cherry Tomato Roast (Page 80)

DAY 6...assuming this is Saturday

***FAMILY EVENT: Head to the local farmer's market and have breakfast there and visit with all the farmers and buy some of your goods for the week!

OR

BREAKFAST
Oatmeal Buttermilk Cinnamon Pancakes (Page 57)
Blueberry Syrup (Page 59)
Don't forget the butter! (Make a double batch and serve the rest on a school day...just pop them in the toaster)
Sausage, bacon or scrambled eggs as a protein side

LUNCH
I'm sure you'll be running errands or going to a game so make it easy on yourself and just grab some good food on the go...but, by all means sit down and eat it and enjoy!

SNACK
Apple with nut butter or nuts (this is a great snack to have in car while running around) or a hunk of cheese

DINNER
Leftover Herbed Meatloaf (Page 105)
Leftover Yukon Gold Potatoes or just boil up some Yukons with sea salt, strain, add a generous

serving of butter, bit of cream and sea salt and pepper and mash away...couldn't be easier!
Leftover Sweet Red Onion Green Beans (Page 78)

DAY 7

BREAKFAST
Blueberry Blast Smoothie (Page 60)

LUNCH
Big salad with two boiled eggs and homemade dressing
Whole-grain crackers
           OR
Leftover Chicken Sausage and Peppers
Yellow Squash & Dill Butter –
Here's what you do:
4 medium-sized yellow crookneck squash, sliced into ¼" half-moons sautéed with "leftover" dill butter from the salmon recipe used earlier in the week. Saute the squash for 4-5 minutes over medium heat, salt and pepper to taste...so easy!

SNACK
Cheesy Popcorn (Page 126)

DINNER
Mediterranean Fish Casserole (Page 115)
Kale with Honey-Lemon Dressing (Page 82)
Whole-grain baguette with butter!

WEEK ONE SHOPPING LIST

PRODUCE

2 heads of garlic
5 lemons
1 bunch of dill or 2 plastic packets of it…if not fresh,
then buy dried
2 lbs. of bags or boxes of frozen whole leaf spinach or
chopped anyway you can get it
2 large bunches green asparagus
One bunch of scallions/spring onions
2 medium sweet potatoes
5 onions
1 sweet onion "Vidalia"
2 heads broccoli
2 Fennel bulbs
1 2 lb. bag Organic Carrots or 2 really nice bunches
equaling 2 pounds
1 bunch fresh basil or a little dried if the store doesn't
have it
Celery – organic is preferable
Fresh thyme
1 bunch Italian "flat leaf" parsley
2 lbs. Yukon Gold Potatoes
1 ½ lbs. green beans
2 medium red onions

**Stuff for a big 'ol salad! **
Suggestions:
-   2 heads of lettuce, romaine, red leaf and arugula
-   Tomatoes, if in season
-   Radishes

- Cucumbers
- Celery & carrots which you will have already bought from higher on this list.

Organic Apples… for snacking
Bananas
Frozen organic blueberries
Local strawberries when they come into season…same for fresh blueberries!
Bell Peppers -- two red and two green and one yellow
4 medium zucchini
4 cups cherry tomatoes
1 lb Kale (about 2 small bunches)

FATS

1 lb. Real butter and "organic" is preferable
Flax seed oil – "Barleans" in refrigerator section at grocery store or health food store
Extra-Virgin Olive Oil
Virgin Coconut Oil – will most likely be found at health food store

SPICES/DRY GOODS

Sea Salt – Celtic brand, gray, fine ground at health food store…buy it in the bag
- some other options: Trader Joe's coarse sea salt from Noirmoutier, Real Salt in a bag - pink in color
- or Hain's sea salt
Pepper Grinder and pepper corns to have fresh ground pepper for recipes
Oatmeal – rolled oats…just like Quaker "Old Fashioned" or Organic rolled oats in bulk section of health food store

Raisins – organic because they're heavily sprayed at least 1 cup

Dried cranberries or dried blueberries – ½ cup for granola recipe

Cinnamon

Pure Maple Syrup

Ground Cumin

Desiccated/unsweetened Coconut (you might find it at a grocer but, definitely at a health food store

Pure Vanilla Extract

1 cup oat flour **or** whole wheat flour – (health food store for the oat flour and grocery store for whole-wheat flour)

All-purpose flour – small package

Paprika

Smoked Paprika by McCormick Spices

Little bit of Cayenne if you decide to use in chicken dish

Quinoa – one box of regular brown variety in grocer or health food store (Quinoa is pronounced "keen-wa"…just so you know)

Dried oregano and thyme

Sucanat –will most likely find this at the local health food store (also goes by names: Rapadura and evaporated cane juice)

Baking powder

Baking soda

Organic corn – for popping

Honey

DAIRY

1 pint Whipping Cream
32 oz. Plain full-fat yogurt with no added sugar,
    organic preferably
Buttermilk – one quart
½ lb. block Colby/Jack cheese
1 block of feta cheese
Parmesan Cheese

MEAT/FISH/EGGS

4 Wild-caught Alaskan Salmon Filets
Bacon with no nitrates and nitrites – see eating plan
    notes, Niman Ranch, etc.
Ground sausage patties with no nitrates and nitrites –
    Niman Ranch or Jones Dairy Farm in freezer
    section or check with your local farmers.
1   3 ½ - 4 ½ lb. whole chicken or cut into pieces
Deli Meats – ham, turkey…no nitrites and nitrates
    (good choices: Applegate Farms, Wellshire Farms,
    Hormel Natural Choice, Boar's Head "Natural")
1 dozen eggs for recipes and more if you're eating for
    breakfast, etc. (buy first at farmers market then
    "organic free-range" at store)
2 lbs. grass-fed ground beef (buy this at the grocery
    store or preferably at the farmer's market)
2 lbs. cooked chicken sausage (or raw from farmers
    market)
1 ½ lbs. white fish like cod, halibut

CAN GOODS

2 15oz. cans garbanzo beans/chick peas
1 16oz. jar of roasted red peppers or roast your own!
2 cans wild-caught salmon for your salads
1 quart canned or boxed chicken broth or make your
    own!
1 --28oz. can diced organic tomatoes
1 can Whole Coconut Milk – found in Thai food
    section with no added sugar! --brands to buy: Thai
    Kitchen, Native Forest and Whole Foods brand
1 jar of fresh salsa…better yet, make your own!

BREAD/RICE/NUTS/SEEDS

Whole golden flax seeds (you'll need a coffee grinder
    to grind them)
***When buying nuts make sure they are raw and
toast them yourselves or buy only roasted with
salt…no added oils…read all labels:
Pecans
Walnuts
Almonds – whole for snacking
Slivered Almonds – 1 cup
Sunflower seeds – 1 cup
Pumpkin seeds
Cashews – Planters has a nice bagged cashew that is
    just roasted and salted
Organic Peanut Butter – Smucker's Organic
Almond Butter – 1 cup
Tahini – ground sesame seeds/paste should be only
    ingredient (this can be found in the ethnic section
    of grocery store)
Ezekiel or Alvarado St. Bakery Bread in frozen health
    food section of grocery store

8 small tortillas or 4 - 10 inch whole-grain tortillas or 100% corn

Whole-grain crackers with no partially-hydrogenated oils at all! Like: Ak Mak, Kavli, Ry-vita, Wasa…all at grocery store

CONDIMENTS

Bragg's Raw Apple Cider Vinegar

Balsamic Vinegar – small bottle

Dijon mustard – Koops, Westbrae or Annies

Mayonnaise – homemade or "Hain" Safflower
  --to be honest, I don't like recommending a mayonnaise because of all the bad fats & other ingredients they use.

Organic Ketchup – Muir Glen or Seeds of Change in health food section of grocery store

"Smoked" Chipotle Tabasco Sauce – grocery store next to regular Tabasco

Pitted Kalamata olives from the "olive bar" at grocer or health food store

All-fruit jam…Organic Smuckers

Sauerkraut -- Ingredients should say: cabbage, salt, water…that's it! Not vinegar because then it would mean that it was pickled…very different animal. This great fermented vegetable, sauerkraut, is so good to have 2-3 tablespoons of especially when you're eating meat because the "good bacteria" and enzymes present in real sauerkraut helps your body break down the protein. Eat it along with your meal and you'll feel great and I bet the kids will love it too!

Bubbies is one that I recommend in the fridge section at your health food store.

"14 Days of Eating in a Real Food Way"

WEEK TWO

DAY 1

BREAKFAST
*Note to self: Don't forget to soak your grits the night before…just refer to the attached recipe.
Cheese-Grits Bowl (Page 62)
And all the fixin's!

LUNCH
Leftover "Mediterranean Fish Casserole"
Whole-grain crackers

SNACK
Smoked Salmon Dill Dip (Page 128)
Crackers or whole-wheat pita chips

DINNER
Rosemary-Lemon Chicken with Roasted Carrots and New Potatoes (Page 109)
Strawberry, Arugula-Romaine Salad with Fennel & toasted sunflower seeds (Page 84)
Strawberry Dressing (Page 136)

*Be sure to soak 2 cups of brown rice while preparing dinner since you'll be cooking it tomorrow night. (Brown Rice Recipe Page 131)

DAY 2

BREAKFAST
Leftover "Oatmeal Pancakes" with "Blueberry Syrup" (pop them in the toaster)
OR
Scramble some eggs in coconut oil and serve with whole-grain toast

LUNCH
Chef Salad with homemade Honey-Balsamic Vinaigrette (Page 134)
Toasted Sunflower Seeds
*Do yourself a favor and make a big salad early in the week that you can eat on for the next 3 days and make enough dressing for the entire week. To keep the salad, spread a damp paper towel over the top of the salad and seal the bowl with plastic wrap.
Whole-grain crackers

SNACK
"Almond Joy" Cookies (Page 129)

DINNER
Salmon with Herbed-Cream Sauce (Page 117)
Sautéed Broccoli-Rabe-Rapini or Swiss Chard (Page 86)
Brown Rice cooked in chicken broth (Page 131)
*Double amount in brown rice recipe to two cups so you can reserve at least 2 cups cooked for Day 5's dinner you should have soaked rice from last night.

DAY 3

BREAKFAST
Strawberry Muffins (Page 64)
Easy-bake sausage (Page 54)

LUNCH
Sandwich with whole-grain bread and leftover
"Rapini or Swiss Chard"
*I recommend Ezekiel or Alvarado St. Bakery because they have the least "tragic" ingredients. Both of these breads and others can be found in most grocery stores in the frozen "health food" bread section. Toasting this bread makes it taste a whole lot better.
*Buy deli meats with no nitrates or nitrites (these are preservatives and believed to cause cancer...so why chance it?). Or you can just make your own deli meat such as, chicken and turkey breast and then you know what you're getting.

*Recommended deli meats:
Wellshire Farm Products
Applegate Farms
Hormel Natural Choice
Boar's Head "Natural" line

SNACK
Apple with cheese or nuts

DINNER
Carrot Soup a la Mexico (Page 139)
Roasted Chicken and Cheese Quesadillas (Page 103)

*plain or with smoky paprika on whole-grain or corn tortillas with fresh or store-bought salsa
*You can use leftover chicken from Day 1's dinner...or a rotisserie chicken from the store, just make sure you shred it.
A little side salad with homemade dressing

***Don't forget to soak your oats for tomorrow morning's breakfast.

DAY 4

BREAKFAST
Blueberry Oatmeal & Nuts
This means just use your recipe on page 52 for the basic "oatmeal" and add fresh blueberries to the oatmeal while it's cooking if you want blue oatmeal or just serve them on top after the oatmeal has cooked...or just serve a small dish of blueberries with a little cream poured on top on the side.

LUNCH
Salad with leftover chicken & Creamy Herb Dressing (page 117)
or Strawberry Dressing (page 136)

SNACK
Full-fat plain yogurt sweetened with a little pure maple syrup, fresh berries in-season and chopped nuts

DINNER

Eggplant Parmesan (Page 99)
Sautéed Collard Greens and Mushrooms (Page 89)
Whole-grain sourdough (if possible) baguette with butter!

DAY 5

BREAKFAST
Scrambled Cheese Eggs and Toast

LUNCH
Deviled Tomatoes (Page 91)
With sliced turkey and some leftover collard greens

SNACK
Smoked-salmon dip with celery sticks

DINNER
Peas and Rice with Kielbasa to boot! (Page 111)
Broccoli with Mushrooms & Roasted Red Peppers (Page 93)
Sliced tomatoes with fresh chopped basil and olive oil

DAY 6...assuming this is Saturday

***FAMILY EVENT: Head to the local farmer's market and have breakfast there and visit with all the farmers and buy some of your goods for the week!

OR

BREAKFAST
Sweet Potato Lamb Hash (Page 67)
Fresh Strawberries and Cream

LUNCH
I'm sure you'll be running errands or going to a game so make it easy on yourself and just grab some good food on the go...but, by all means sit down and eat it and enjoy!

SNACK
Blueberry Blast Smoothie (Page 60)
Whole-grain crackers and nut butter

DINNER
Time to grill out!
Hamburgers (made with a combo of grass-fed beef & lamb or pork)
You can find all these great meats at your local farmer's market.
Preparing the hamburger patties: form the meat loosely into patties, salt and pepper liberally,

sprinkle with a little smoked paprika on each side and grill...and cheese is always a good addition. ☺

Whole-grain buns

Sweet & Sour Cole Slaw (Page 95)
Grilled Rosemary Squash (Page 97)

DAY 7

BREAKFAST
Squash Frittata (Page 69)
Whole-grain toast with butter & fruit spread

LUNCH
Sandwich with "good" deli meats & leftover "Sweet & Sour Cole Slaw"

SNACK
Cheesy Popcorn cooked with coconut oil and sprinkle a little smoked paprika for fun! (Page 126)

DINNER
Out to dinner!

OR

Coconut Shrimp Soup with Noodles (Page 119)
Sautéed Snap Peas & Red Peppers (Page 98)

OR

Just have a smorgasbord of leftovers from the week! ☺

WEEK TWO SHOPPING LIST

PRODUCE

1 big bunch dill
1-2 big bunches of Basil
4 lemons
1 bunch fresh Rosemary
1 bunch fresh Italian "Flat Leaf" Parsley
1 bunch fresh thyme
Fresh tarragon (just a bit)
2 lbs. small-medium new potatoes
1 pound carrots (8-10 medium)
1 large bunch or plastic container of pre-washed
    arugula
1 small head, romaine lettuce
1 fennel bulb, medium size
1 bunch organic celery (because the conventional is
    very heavily sprayed with pesticides)
Fresh Strawberries galore from the local farmer's
    market
Fresh Chives
2 big bunches Broccoli Rabe (Rapini) leafy green with
    little broccoli tops
3 lbs. whole carrots, organic preferably (you'll use 2
    lbs. in the carrot soup)
5 onions
1 Vidalia onion
2 bunches spring/green onions…scallions
2 heads fresh garlic
One bunch fresh cilantro
2 large bunches collard greens or kale
8 ounces shiitake mushrooms or Baby Bella's thinly
    sliced

1 8 ounce package sliced button mushrooms
1 green pepper
1 cucumber
6 small tomatoes or 6 large Roma tomatoes…more
   for slicing as a side dish!
2 cups fresh Purple Hull or Crowder Peas (in season)
2 bunches broccoli
2 medium sweet potatoes
1 small head white cabbage
1 small head red cabbage
6 medium yellow "crook neck" summer squash
1 medium zucchini
Small 2" piece fresh ginger
2 limes
¾ lb. sugar snap peas
2 small red bell peppers
2 lbs. eggplant

FATS

Flax seed oil – "Barleans" in refrigerator section at
   grocery store or health food store
Extra-Virgin Olive Oil
Virgin - Unrefined Coconut Oil – will most likely be
   found at health food store
Unrefined/Expeller pressed sesame oil
Toasted sesame oil (small bottle)

SPICES/DRY GOODS

Unsweetened Cocoa Powder
White Balsamic Vinegar
Organic medium or fine-ground grits (not instant grits,
   please)

Sea Salt – Celtic brand, gray, fine ground at health food store…buy it in the bag

--some other options: Trader Joe's coarse sea salt from Noirmoutier, Real Salt in a bag it's pink in color or Hain's sea salt

Pepper Grinder and pepper corns to have fresh ground pepper for recipes

Oatmeal – rolled oats…just like Quaker "Old Fashioned" oats -- or organic rolled oats in bulk section of health food store

Cinnamon

Nutmeg…just a little

Pure Maple Syrup

Ground Cumin

Desiccated/unsweetened Coconut (maybe at a grocer but, definitely at a health food store

Pure Vanilla Extract

Whole-wheat flour – small package

Long-grain brown rice

Sucanat/Rapadura or evaporated whole cane sugar – will most likely find this at the local health food store

Baking powder

Baking soda

Organic corn – for popping

Honey

Celery seed – ½ teaspoon

Thai Kitchen Premium Fish Sauce

Thai Kitchen Roasted Red Chili Paste

DAIRY – Buy organic when possible.

1 lb. Real Butter
Cheddar Cheese
Large container plain Greek yogurt
Goat Cheese
Sour cream (small container)
Buttermilk
Full-fat plain yogurt
Parmesan Reggiano
2 lbs. whole milk ricotta

MEAT/FISH/EGGS

One 4 ounce package smoked salmon in seafood
    section of grocer
One 3 ½ - 4 lb. whole chicken or cut into pieces
    (hormone & antibiotic free)
4 Wild-caught Alaskan Salmon Filets – freezer section
    of any grocery store
1 ¼ lbs. wild-caught shrimp frozen or fresh
Bacon with no nitrates and nitrites – see eating plan
    notes, Niman Ranch, etc.
Ground sausage patties with no nitrates and nitrites –
    Niman Ranch or Jones Dairy Farm in freezer
    section or farmer's market
Deli Meats – ham, turkey…no nitrites and nitrates
    (good choices: Applegate Farms, Wellshire Farms,
    Hormel Natural Choice, Boar's Head "Natural")
2 dozen eggs for recipes and more if you're eating for
    breakfast, etc. (buy first at farmers market then
    "organic free-range" at store)
1 lb. grass-fed ground beef (buy this at the grocery
    store or preferably at the farmer's market)
1 lb. ground pork

½ pound smoked turkey kielbasa (next to the hot dogs) no nitrites/nitrates please.
1 lb. ground lamb or ground pork for "sweet potato lamb hash recipe"...so just use whichever you prefer

CAN GOODS

2 cans wild-caught salmon for your salads
3 quarts canned or boxed chicken broth or make your own!
Whole Coconut Milk – 1 can or more for smoothies can be found in Thai food section with no added sugar!--brands to buy: Thai Kitchen, Native Forest and Whole Foods brand
1 jar of fresh salsa
1 large jar organic marinara sauce (2 cups/16 oz. at least)

BREAD/RICE/NUTS/SEEDS

Brown Rice – long grain (at least 2 cups)
Whole golden flax seeds (you'll need a coffee grinder to grind them)
***When buying nuts make sure they are raw and toast them yourselves or buy only roasted with salt...no added oils...read all labels:
Almonds – 1 cup -- whole/raw for "Almond Joy" Cookies
Slivered Almonds – 1 cup
Sunflower seeds – 1 cup
Sesame seeds – 2 teaspoons
Ezekiel or Alvarado St. Bakery Bread in frozen health food section of grocery store

8 small 100% corn tortillas or four 10 inch whole-grain
   tortillas (sprouted, if at all possible)
Whole-grain crackers with no partially-hydrogenated
   oils at all! Like: Ak Mak, Kavli, Ry-vita, Wasa…all
   at grocery store
Whole-grain baguette – wait to buy fresh for the day
   when cooking Eggplant Parmesan

CONDIMENTS

Soy Sauce – Naturally fermented with no MSG or
   caramel coloring in ingredients…San-J is a "good"
   brand
Bragg's Raw Apple Cider Vinegar
Capers – in the jarred pickle area of your grocery
   store
Dijon mustard – Koops, Westbrae or Annies
Mayonnaise – homemade or "Hain" Safflower --to be
   honest, I don't like recommending a mayonnaise
   because of all the bad fats & other ingredients
   they use.
All-fruit jam like Organic Smuckers
Sauerkraut -- Ingredients should say: cabbage, salt,
   water…that's it! Not vinegar because then it
   would mean that it was pickled…very different
   animal. This great fermented vegetable,
   sauerkraut, is so good to have 2-3 tablespoons of
   especially when you're eating meat because the
   "good bacteria" and enzymes present in real
   sauerkraut helps your body break down the
   protein. Eat it along with your meal and you'll feel
   great and I bet the kids will love it too!

Bubbies is one I recommend and can be found in the
   fridge section at your health food store.

RECIPES

BREAKFAST

QUICK-COOKING REAL OATMEAL
Yield: Serves 4

We all know about the goodness of oatmeal, right? So now I want you to throw away all the other "versions" of oatmeal in your pantry...especially the instant variety. In this very simple oatmeal recipe I will give you a few tips to make that porridge the yummiest you and your kids have ever had and it will cook in about three minutes! First, you want to soak your oatmeal in the water it will be cooked in overnight with a little lemon juice. The acid starts to break down and pre-digest the grain so that it cooks in no time and more importantly it's easier for your digestive system to break it down and make the nutrients more available to your body. Traditional cultures would have never dreamed of eating grains that had not been soaked/fermented in some way before cooking them. The only thing you have to remember is to soak your oats the night before you want to cook them. That seems easy enough, right?

Ingredients:
2 cups rolled oats
4 cups water
2 teaspoons fresh lemon juice
½ teaspoon sea salt
1 teaspoon cinnamon

Procedure:

- The night before you want to eat oatmeal for breakfast place the oats, water and lemon juice into a stainless steel saucepan. Give the oats a quick stir, put a lid on the pot and just set on the countertop until morning. The oats can soak at room temperature for 7-24 hours.
- In the morning add the sea salt and cinnamon and bring the oats to a boil, turn down the heat to a simmer, stir well and then cover and let simmer for about 2 minutes until your desired consistency.
- Now the fun begins...add in any and all of the following items:
    - Real butter and plenty of it!
    - Ground flaxseed if you're so inclined
    - Real cream
    - Pure maple syrup, but only a little...it's still sugar
    - Toasted pecans, walnuts or whatever nuts or seeds you like
    - Raisins or other dried fruit

Notes:

Now this is a breakfast to get everyone firing on all cylinders!

EASY-BAKE SAUSAGE OR BACON

When I'm in a hurry and trying to get out the door in the morning but, still want to eat some good protein for breakfast and I don't have time to nurse a pan of sausage or bacon for 15-20 minutes at the stove then I cook it in the oven. It's such an efficient use of my time.

Here's what you do:

1. Heat the oven to 350°F.
2. Lay a sheet of parchment paper onto a baking sheet and lay out your bacon or raw sausage patties so that "nobody" is touching.
3. Cook for 20-25 minutes total but you'll need to turn your sausage and bacon over halfway through the cooking time.
4. Toast up some whole grain bread and call it breakfast!

EGG AND MUST-GO VEGGIE PIE
Yield: Serves 6

Everybody is in a hurry in the morning, but we've got to eat if we want to have enough energy to conquer all we want to do these days. So, I'm always trying to think of recipes for me and others that will make their lives a little less complicated in the morning when it comes to food and I don't mean cereal. I mean some good protein, carbohydrate and fat, yeah! You put together the egg mixture the night before, so all you have to do is pour it over some cooked veggies and cheese in a pie plate and bake ...throw some cheese on top and call it breakfast!

Whoever gets up first, turn the oven on, put your "pie" together, throw it in the oven, go get ready for the day and breakfast is ready in 25- 30 minutes! And leftovers are great too.

Ingredients:
1-2 cups of leftover cooked veggies like, asparagus, spinach, broccoli, etc.
6 eggs
½ cup full-fat ricotta
¾ teaspoon sea salt
Ground pepper
½ cup crumbled goat cheese
¼ - ½ cup of asiago, cheddar, jack or parmesan cheese on top

Procedure:
1. Preheat the oven to 350°F
2. Butter a glass or ceramic pie plate.

3. Place the veggies evenly on the bottom of the buttered plate and then crumble the goat cheese over the veggies.
4. Whisk together the eggs and ricotta cheese and salt and pepper and pour evenly over the vegetables and goat cheese.
5. Sprinkle the cheese over the egg mixture and bake for 25-30 minutes until a knife inserted in the middle of the pie comes out clean.
6. Let cool for about 5 minutes, run the knife around the edge of the pie to loosen it and serve with some whole-grain toast, butter and real fruit jam.

Notes:
Get your eggs at the local farmers market and enjoy the taste of delicious, fresh eggs!

OATMEAL BUTTERMILK CINNAMON PANCAKES
Yield: 20 (4-inch pancakes)

I love pancakes, but have not loved the way traditionally-made pancakes make me feel…like I've just eaten a candy bar because they are so "refined" and sweet. Soaking the oats in buttermilk overnight helps to break down the oats and make them easier to digest. This hearty pancake recipe helps keep your blood-sugar levels even by using oats as the base and some good fat to boot. You will feel nothing but nourished after eating them even with some "real" blueberry maple syrup drizzled on top! Make these pancakes the new tradition for Saturday mornings.

Ingredients:
2 cups rolled oats
3 cups buttermilk
½ cup whole wheat flour
½ cup all-purpose flour
2 tablespoons Sucanat*
½ teaspoon baking powder
½ teaspoon baking soda
1 teaspoon cinnamon
1/2 teaspoon sea salt
2 large free-range organic eggs, lightly beaten
4 tablespoons unsalted butter, melted and cooled
Butter for the griddle

Procedure:

1. Stir oats into 2 cups buttermilk in a medium bowl and let stand, overnight, covered in the fridge.
2. Whisk together flours, Sucanat (evaporated cane juice), baking powder, baking soda, cinnamon and salt until combined well. In the oat/buttermilk mixture stir in remaining 1 cup buttermilk, eggs until well combined. Stir in the dry ingredients until just blended.
3. Brush a large skillet or griddle with a little butter and heat over moderately high heat until droplets of water scatter over the griddle. Pour the batter onto the griddle by ¼-cup measures and cook pancakes for 1-2 minutes on each side, or until golden, brushing the griddle with some of the melted butter as necessary.
4. Transfer pancakes as they are cooked to a sheet pan and keep warm in a preheated 225° oven. Serve pancakes topped with blueberry syrup. See attached recipe.

*Sucanat is unrefined, evaporated sugar cane juice...with all of its mineral and micronutrients intact. You can purchase Sucanat from a health food store. I always use this in the equal amount that a recipe calls for white sugar.

BLUEBERRY SYRUP

Yields: 1 cup

Sometimes kids can get a little crazy with pouring too much maple syrup on their already sweet pancakes. This recipe for blueberry syrup gives them something sweet and good to pour all over their pancakes without all the sugary sweetness of just plain syrup.

1 (6 oz) container fresh blueberries or 1 cup frozen blueberries
½ cup real maple syrup

Bring blueberries to a simmer in a small saucepan with maple syrup until blueberries burst, mixture is thickened and reduced to 1 cup, about 5-6 minutes. Serve immediately over pancakes or homemade ice cream...yum!

BLUEBERRY BLAST SMOOTHIE

Yield: 3 ½ cups, 2-3 smoothies

Smoothies are a great choice for breakfast when you're in a hurry or for an afternoon pick-me-up for parents and kids. I am not a fan of any "protein powder" not even whey powder. If we only knew the process that protein powders have to go through before we consume them we wouldn't eat them. They are truly denatured and very hard for us to digest by the time we use them. So, I of course recommend you use real-food forms of protein like egg yolks, hemp seeds that you grind at home, nut butters and full-fat plain yogurt. And, always add in some delicious organic berries for their anti-oxidant benefits.

Ingredients:
1 cup full-fat plain yogurt
1 cup unsweetened canned coconut milk*
1 cup frozen blueberries or some other berry
2-3 raw egg yolks**
1 teaspoon cinnamon
2 tablespoons pure maple syrup

Procedure:
1. Place all the ingredients in a blender and mix on the high setting until all the fruit is pureed, 3-4 minutes. Add in some ice if you want your smoothie a little more frozen.

Notes:

*Canned coconut milk can be found in any grocery store in the "Thai" food section. The "whole fat" version is what you want with no added sugars. You may need to open the can and scoop it into a bowl to whisk because the coconut fat likes to rise to the top in some brands. Coconut fat is so very good for you because it has immune-boosting properties and half of it is burned by your body for energy.

Only eat raw egg yolks if you buy your eggs **fresh from a local farmer or at the farmers market and you know that they raise healthy, happy chickens. You have a much better chance of getting salmonella from under-cooked eggs from factory-raised chickens that have never seen the light of day and they are much less nutritious in my opinion. Plus, the factory eggs are irradiated before they hit the stores depleting their original-intended goodness just one more time. And, it has been proven that eggs are not a culprit in raising our blood cholesterol...they are perfectly great for you and your eyesight and they are the perfect protein...now that's real food!

CHEDDAR CHEESE GRITS BOWL
Yield: Serves 4-6

Comfort food equals cheese grits for a lot of Southerners…especially this one! It's the starch staple of the South. Nothing complicated about this recipe. I suggest soaking the grits over night because it decreases the cooking time and pre-digests the grain making it easier for you to digest. And remember you can't get all the goodness of the grits unless you eat some delicious fat with them. The fat also helps to slow down the breakdown of the carbohydrate in your digestive tract which in turn means there will be a smaller spike in your blood sugar level.

Ingredients:
1 cup organic medium or fine-ground grits (no instant grits, please)
4 cups water
1 tablespoon lemon juice
½ teaspoon sea salt
2 tablespoons butter
1 cup grated raw milk cheddar or any other kind of cheese you prefer
More salt to taste
¼ teaspoon fresh ground pepper

Procedure:
1. Soak the grits in the water and lemon juice overnight in a 3-4 quart sauce pan with the lid. Just leave the pan on the counter at room temperature.

2. Put the pan over high heat without the lid and add the salt and butter and bring it to a boil. It's a good idea to whisk the grits while they are coming up to a boil so that they don't clump together.
3. Bring the grits down to a simmer and cover the pot, stirring occasionally for about 15-20 minutes. Or to your desired consistency. Add more water if they get too thick.
4. Now add in the cheese right before serving. Stir it well to make sure all the cheese has melted and serve it up with a few poached/fried eggs on top or some great locally, pasture-raised sausage. And, if you're really feeling daring then serve some sautéed spinach on the serving of grits as well and call it a complete meal!

Special Note:
Right after you've served the grits and there are any leftover then just spread them out in about 1 inch thickness in a container and put them in the fridge. The next day you can just cut them into squares and fry them up in a pan to add to your breakfast, lunch or dinner meal. You gotta love left overs!

STRAWBERRY MUFFINS
Yield: 12 muffins

When strawberries come into season I'm always thinking, "What else can I make with a strawberry?" So here is a delicious and lightly sweetened, 100% whole wheat breakfast or snack bread for the whole family. Just make sure you put a nice slab of butter on it before you eat it because the fat will help keep your blood sugar levels more stable.

Ingredients:
1 ¾ cups sifted whole wheat flour
¼ teaspoon sea salt
2 teaspoons baking powder
½ teaspoon baking soda
½ teaspoon cinnamon
¼ teaspoon ground nutmeg
½ cup sucanat (organic whole cane sugar)*
1/3 cup coconut oil**
2 eggs
1 teaspoon vanilla extract
¾ cup buttermilk
1 cup small chopped fresh strawberries

Procedure:
1. Preheat the oven to 350°F and place paper muffin cups in the pan/s.
2. Melt coconut oil in a small saucepan and set aside.
3. In a large mixing bowl, sift together flour, sea salt, baking powder, baking soda, cinnamon and nutmeg. Create a well in the middle.

4. In a smaller bowl beat together the sucanat, coconut oil, eggs, vanilla and buttermilk and pour into the well of the dry ingredients and stir slowly with a spatula until just mixed. Fold in the fresh strawberries until evenly distributed throughout the dough.
5. Transfer batter to paper muffin cups.
6. Bake until golden brown, 20-25 minutes, until a toothpick inserted in the center comes out clean. Let cool for 5 minutes, then transfer muffins to a wire rack to cool completely.

Notes:

*Sucanat (sugar cane natural) or "organic whole cane sugar" as the package now says is what sucanat is. It is sugar cane juice with all of its goodness and minerals intact that has been dehydrated and grated. You can always use sucanat in equal measure to refined sugar. The difference is in the taste and sucanat tastes and is less sweet than white sugar and you just "feel better" after eating a sweet treat made with sucanat. Some grocery stores are carrying this in their "health food section" otherwise, you'll find it at your local health food store. It's really worth the trip!

**You should be incorporating coconut oil into your diet by now if you're following my eating plan and have it in your cabinet. We all know about the health benefits of coconut oil and it can be used in so many ways...including baking. You only want to buy "unrefined" coconut oil, so just pick this up at the health food store when you get the sucanat. Unless you're making a pastry dough or biscuits you will need to melt the coconut oil and then add it to your recipe.

Also keep in mind if you're making one of your favorite recipes and you want to use coconut oil instead of butter, oil or Crisco then just use 25% less coconut oil than what the original recipe calls for.

SWEET POTATO LAMB HASH

Yield: Serves 6

I stopped eating cereal many years ago and so I'm always looking for more savory and delicious ideas for breakfast. This recipe satisfies my appetite with the lamb, herbs and the divine sweetness of the sweet potatoes. Keep in mind you can serve this at any meal of the day just as you can eat anything for breakfast. I want to know who started this whole sweet breakfast habit anyway? A real tragedy for our society that is for sure! ☺

Ingredients:
2 tablespoons extra-virgin olive oil
2 medium sweet potatoes cut into a ½ inch dice
1 medium onion, cut into ½ inch dice
½ teaspoon dried thyme
½ teaspoon dried oregano
¾ teaspoon sea salt
¼ teaspoon fresh ground black pepper
1 lb ground lamb (ground pork or grass-fed beef will do just fine, too)

Procedure:
1. In a 10-12 inch skillet add the olive oil, potatoes, onion, thyme, oregano, salt and pepper and sauté over medium-high heat for about ten minutes. Then lower the heat to medium and cook for another five minutes.
2. Remove the sweet potato mixture from the pan and set it aside and cover it to keep it warm.

3. Place the ground lamb into the pan over medium heat and continue to break it apart with a spatula until it is crumbled and browned through.
4. When the lamb is cooked through then strain off all of the fat in the bottom of the pan.
5. Add the sweet potato mixture to the lamb in the pan and cook it over medium-low heat for another 5 minutes. Season it with more salt and pepper if need be and it's all ready.

Note:
Serve this with a nice green vegetable and a fruit and your meal is complete!

SUMMER SQUASH FRITTATA

Yield: Serves 4-6

This is just another way to use all that fabulous summer squash that really seems to be in abundance by June and July. The best eggs are your local, pasture-raised farm-fresh eggs. This is also a great way to use up any leftover veggies you have in the fridge. Best of all this meal comes together in no time and don't forget a nice big salad or serving of broccoli on the side with butter! And this makes a great summer supper, too.

Ingredients:
1 ½ cups zucchini chopped into ½ inch pieces
1 ½ cups yellow squash chopped into ½ inch pieces
    (Or just use 3 cups of any raw veggies you might
    have in the fridge, or 2 cups cooked veggies)
2 tablespoons organic butter or unrefined coconut oil
¾ teaspoon sea salt
¼ teaspoon ground pepper
8 eggs whisked thoroughly
2 tablespoons fresh tarragon or some other herb
    finely chopped
½ cup parmesan cheese grated or whatever cheese
    you like

Procedure:
1. Preheat the oven to broil.
2. In a medium bowl whisk the eggs with the chopped tarragon or other herbs, sea salt, fresh ground pepper and set aside.
3. In a large oven-proof skillet over medium heat add the butter or coconut oil. Add the

squashes, season with a few good pinches of salt and some fresh cracked pepper and sauté stirring occasionally until everything is cooked through, about 5-7 minutes. If the veggies produce a bit of water then press the squashes a bit and pour it out of the pan before adding the eggs.

4. Pour the eggs evenly over the veggies. As the edges start to set lift them up and let some of the eggs run underneath the frittata to cook for about 3 minutes and then sprinkle the grated cheese over the top

5. Place the pan about 6 inches from the broiler and finish cooking the frittata until the eggs on top are set...for about 2 minutes.

6. Let it cool for a few minutes and then cut it into wedges and serve. This is one of those dishes that is good hot or at room temperature. A little salsa on top makes a nice addition!

VEGETABLES

CREAMED SPINACH
Yield: Serves 6-8

I love creamed spinach, just not swimming in the cream. So here we have a simple creamed spinach recipe with "enough" cream to make this side dish very satisfying. I buy the frozen whole leaf organic spinach, but any old kind will do.

Ingredients:
3 cloves garlic, coarsely chopped
1 tablespoon olive oil
1 tablespoon butter
2 – 16 oz (1lb.) bags whole leaf spinach thawed, water squeezed out a bit and coarsely chopped
¼ teaspoon sea salt and more to taste
Ground pepper
¼ cup "real" cream

Procedure:
1. Using a 12" skillet over medium heat melt the butter into the olive oil and then add the chopped garlic and sauté for about 2 minutes.
2. Add in the spinach, salt and pepper and stir everything together well and cook for 6-7 minutes until the spinach is done or to the consistency you like.
3. Add in the cream and stir well turning the heat down to medium low and cooking the spinach for another 2 minutes…then serve.
4. If you like more cream, then by all means, add more!

Notes:

You can go the fresh spinach route on this but I prefer to keep the really fresh spring spinach for a nice salad. Keep in mind you must eat good fats with your veggies to be able to absorb all those great, necessary for good health, fat-soluble vitamins, A, K, D & E! Spinach is a good source of vitamins A and K. Also, if you have leftovers then be sure to toss it into some eggs for an omelette or my "Egg and Must-Go Veggie Pie" later in the week.

ROASTED ASPARAGUS
Yield: Serves 6-8

In the spring just pray that a farmer near you grows asparagus. If you've never had it fresh from the farm then all I can say is get it and eat as much of it as you can because it's growing season is quite short. And because it is so delicious and fresh then it should only be cooked briefly and simply, I think.

Ingredients:
2 big bunches of fresh asparagus, washed and dried well
2 tablespoons extra virgin olive oil
¼ teaspoon sea salt
Ground pepper

Procedure:
1. Heat oven to 425℉
2. Place the clean, dry asparagus on the roasting pan in a single layer. Drizzle the olive oil over the asparagus and salt and pepper. Toss the asparagus to make sure they are all coated with oil.
3. Roast for 5-8 minutes until your desired doneness. Keep in mind they will keep cooking once you take the asparagus out of the oven.

Notes:
IF there are any leftovers then be sure to throw them into an omelette or "Egg and Must-Go Veggie Pie" later in the week.

BROTH-STEAMED BROCCOLI

Yield: Serves 4-6

Sometimes you just need a little green something to go with your meal, right? Green is good. Anyway, I love anything green braised or steamed in chicken broth. Homemade chicken broth is the best but, store bought will do…just read the ingredients. There should be "no sugar" in your chicken broth that is for sure. Or you cannot get frustrated with trying to find a "good" chicken stock and just use water.

Ingredients:
2 lbs. broccoli
2 tablespoons butter
2 tablespoons extra-virgin olive oil
Chicken broth or water
¼ tsp. sea salt
Ground pepper

Procedure:
1. Wash and cut the florets off of the broccoli stalk…leaving some stem on the floret
2. In an 8 quart stock pot over medium heat melt the butter into the olive oil then add in the broccoli, and enough stock/water to come up about ¼" on the side of the pan.
3. Bring to a boil, turn heat down to medium and stir the broccoli well, put the lid on and cook 4-5 minutes until the broccoli is just tender. Add in the salt and pepper.
4. Turn off the heat – cover again and let sit for a minute.
5. Serve it up with a little parmesan cheese.

Notes:

This is a great basic recipe for cooking hearty greens like Kale and Collard Greens or the more delicate Swiss Chard.

OVEN-ROASTED YUKON GOLD POTATOES

Yield: Serves 6-8

Did you know the average American eats about 1 potato a day? Wow, that is something. So instead of fried, here is an oven-roasted potato that is so creamy and delicious.

Ingredients:
2 lbs. Yukon Gold Potatoes
1 tablespoon coconut oil
2 tablespoons butter
Sea salt and ground pepper

Procedure:
1. Heat oven to 350°F
2. Melt the coconut oil and butter in a small saucepan.
3. Wash and dry the potatoes and cut them into 1" X 2" chunks.
4. Place the potatoes onto a large baking sheet and pour the oil/butter mixture over the potatoes and toss on the sheet until they are well coated. And make sure they are all spread out and not piled on to one another.
5. Bake for about one hour and turn them every 20 minutes.
6. When just out of the oven season them with sea salt and ground pepper.

Notes:
You always want to make sure you eat a good amount of fat with potatoes because the fat will help to slow the absorption of the glucose into your

bloodstream...therefore preventing a spike in your blood sugar levels. Plus eating potatoes with some protein is advisable too. Remember, it's all about balance...every time you eat something make sure there is a good balance of protein, fat and carbohydrate, your body will thank you!

* If serving these potatoes with the meatloaf, and you only have one oven, then put them on the shelf below the meatloaf and cook them at the same time!

SWEET RED ONION GREEN BEANS

Yield: 6 servings

Ingredients:

1 ½ pounds green beans, ends removed and snapped into 2-3 inch pieces
2 tablespoons extra virgin olive oil
1 tablespoon butter
1 large red onion cut in half and then into ¼ inch half-moon slices
3 tablespoons balsamic vinegar
¼ teaspoon sea salt
Fresh ground pepper to taste
½ cup crumbled feta cheese

Procedure:

1. In a pot of boiling, salted (1 tablespoon for every four quarts of water) water cook green beans 3-4 minutes...cooked a bit, but still crisp. Drain the beans and spread them out onto a cookie sheet to cool.
2. In a large skillet over medium-high heat add the olive oil and butter.
3. Sauté the red onions with a few shakes of sea salt and cook for about 5 minutes or until onions are limp and cooked through.
4. Turn the heat to medium and add the balsamic vinegar and cook another minute.
5. Add blanched green beans and sauté for 3-5 minutes more.
6. Remove the green beans from the heat and season with salt and fresh ground pepper.
7. Crumble feta cheese all over green beans before serving.

Note:
- You can serve this dish hot or at room temperature...both are delicious and nutritious!
- "Half-moon slices" means that you cut against the grain of the onion...not with it. Some call this the "salad slice."

ZUCCHINI, CHERRY TOMATO ROAST
Yield: Serves 6-8

What a classic little Italian combo, zucchini and tomatoes…you could make this a million different ways to Sunday. But, let's just keep this simple especially when zucchini and tomatoes are in season, oh my, they are both so sweet and delicious.

Ingredients:
4 medium zucchini, quartered and cut into 2 inch long
    pieces
2 cups cherry tomatoes cut in half or quarter 4-5 plum
    tomatoes, then cut in half
¼ teaspoon sea salt & more to taste
1/8 teaspoon ground pepper
2 tablespoons extra-virgin olive oil
Freshly grated parmesan cheese

Procedure:
1. Place the oven rack in the upper third of the oven and turn on the broiler.
2. Using a roasting pan/sheet place the cut zucchini and tomatoes, sprinkle the salt and pepper and drizzle the extra virgin olive oil all over the veggies and toss with your hands until the veggies are evenly coated and settled into one layer with the whites of the zucchini facing up.
3. Broil for 10-12 minutes stirring half-way through the cooking time. Remove from the oven and serve with some fresh grated parmesan cheese…delightful!

Notes:

Any leftovers can be served at breakfast as a side, small chop it and add it to your eggs, serve at room temperature as a salad with some fresh mozzarella and basil added in! Now you're talking summer!

KALE WITH HONEY-LEMON DRESSING
Yield: 6-8 Servings

We've all heard about how good it is to eat lots of dark greens and that is the honest truth. For instance, there is an almost equal serving of calcium in a cup of greens as there is in a glass of milk. Not to mention all the other nutrients like lutein and vitamin A that are so great for your eyes. Just remember, it's hard to assimilate all the goodness of greens unless we eat "good" fat with them. Just try and eat something dark green every day and feel the difference. Depending on where you live, fresh dark leafy greens might only available in the cooler months, early fall to late spring. So stock up!

To Cook Kale:
1 pound kale (2 small bunches), chopped into bite-sized pieces and washed*
1 cup water
½ teaspoon sea salt & more to taste

Honey-Lemon Dressing:
1 tablespoon honey
2 tablespoons fresh lemon juice
1 teaspoon ground cumin
½ cup extra-virgin olive oil
¼ teaspoon sea salt
Ground pepper
½ cup crumbled feta cheese
Toasted pine nuts or sunflower seeds

Procedure:

1. In a large sauté pan over high heat bring kale, water and salt to a boil. Lower heat to medium-high, put on lid and cook for 12 minutes stirring occasionally.
2. While the kale is cooking in a small bowl mix together honey, lemon juice, cumin, olive oil, salt and pepper and set aside.
3. Taste the kale for doneness. Cook another 5 minutes without the lid if need be. Drain off any water left in the pan and spread kale onto a serving platter.
4. Mix the dressing really well and pour all over the kale and toss until the greens are coated. Sprinkle the feta all over the greens and some toasted pine nuts or sunflower seeds if you're so inclined.

Notes:

*Here's what I do to wash big bunches of hearty greens like kale and collards: I take the biggest bowl I have or a "clean" sink and fill with cold water. Put chopped greens in cold water and actively toss them around in the water "washing" them and then let them set for a few minutes to let any sand fall away from the greens. Lift the greens out of the water and then they are ready to cook.

STRAWBERRY SALAD
Yield: 4-6 servings

Strawberries in season are too fabulous for words! So, I try and put them into everything I can and eat them all the time. Thinly sliced fennel adds a nice little sweet crunch to this salad. And, what else would you put on a Strawberry Salad but Strawberry Vinaigrette? Spring and fall are the best times to buy any type of lettuce so eat lots of salads before the summer heat wilts the lettuces.

Ingredients:
4 cups arugula* washed and dried in a salad
      spinner**
4 cups romaine lettuce torn into bite-sized pieces,
      washed and dried
½ fennel bulb, medium-sized, thinly sliced equal to 1
      & ½ cups***
2 celery stalks thinly sliced on the diagonal equal to ¾
      cup
1 cup ¼ inch vertical slices, fresh strawberries
½ cup crumbled goat cheese
¼ cup toasted sunflower seeds****

Procedure:

1. In a large salad bowl mix the washed greens together.
2. Layer the salad in this order: lettuces, fennel, celery, strawberries, goat cheese and sunflower seeds.
3. Serve it up and then drizzle Strawberry Vinaigrette onto each serving.

*Arugula is a peppery/little bitter tasting leafy vegetable. Because of the bitter aspect it actually aids in digestion. Most grocery stores sell arugula.
**Salad Spinner – if you don't have one of these then by all means make your life a whole lot easier and get one. I recommend the OXO brand.
***Fennel – also known as Sweet or Florence Fennel is a white bulb with hollow stalks with leafy green fronds. Fennel has a wonderful sweet licorice flavor and it is good raw or cooked. To prepare it cut off the hollow stalks, wash the bulb well, cut down the middle and then slice.
****To toast sunflower seeds: buy plain un-toasted sunflower seeds, place them in a small sauté pan and over medium heat toast them for about 4-5 minutes, moving them every 30 seconds or so. When they become fragrant then put them on a plate to cool before adding to the salad.

BRAISED BROCCOLI RABE (RAPINI)
Yield: Serves 4-6

You know all those crazy eating contests, people making themselves sick on consuming hotdogs, doughnuts, pie, etc.? Well, I think we should have an eating contest in the spring and early summer to see who can consume the most braised/sautéed GREENS like collard greens, kale (Russian Red Leaf, Lecanto, and curly leaf), Swiss chard, Broccoli, Rapini, you get the idea! Talk about nutritious overload. Greens are loaded with minerals, vitamins and anti-oxidants. The one that really blew me away is that one serving of kale or collards has about the same amount of calcium as you would get in a glass of milk! So, I don't guess it would surprise you to know that my husband, Alex and I even eat them for breakfast, with good ol' southern pepper vinegar, of course. Broccoli Rabe (Rapini) is a little more bitter than the others mentioned above so the braising helps to soften that, but it's delicious and has great flavor! Keep in mind that when foods are a little bitter they aid in the digestion of other foods by getting our body's to produce more gastric juices to break food down.

Ingredients:
2 big bunches Broccoli Rabe (Rapini)* 3-4" of stems
    removed, cut into bite-sized pieces & wash
2 tablespoons butter
2 tablespoons extra-virgin olive oil
4 garlic cloves coarsely chopped
1 cup chicken broth/stock
1 teaspoon sea salt

¼ teaspoon ground pepper

Procedure:
1. Soak and wash the cut Broccoli Rabe in a big bowl of water and then lift them out into another clean bowl and set aside.
2. In a deep-sided sauté pan over medium heat sauté the butter, olive oil and garlic for 2 minutes and add in the broth. Add in the greens, salt, pepper and stir well so that all the greens are starting to wilt and stock is boiling.
3. Bring heat down to a simmer, put lid on and braise** for 15 minutes stirring every 4-5 minutes.
4. Serve with a drizzle of flax seed oil*** & a few little splashes of pepper vinegar.

Notes:

*Broccoli Rabe (Rapini) can be found in your local grocery store or at the farmer's market in season, spring, early summer and fall.
**Braising is a wonderful way to cook heartier greens. Using a liquid that only comes up 1/3 of the way of the food, with the lid on the food can cook in its own juices for a more concentrated and delicious flavor and creating a more tender green in the end.
***Drizzling some flax seed oil on your cooked greens just boosts the nutritional value because it is an essential fatty acid/Omega -3 which fights inflammation and boosts brain power. And, eating fat with any greens helps your body assimilate the fat soluble vitamins (A, D, K & E). Just remember to never cook with flax seeds or flax seed oil because the higher heat will destroy all that is good about the

oil since it is a delicate polyunsaturated oil and goes rancid easily. When buying look for the cold-pressed, unfiltered in a dark plastic bottle, like Barleans. Be sure to check the expiration date because you want to buy the freshest so that you can to get the best benefit.

SAUTEED COLLARDS AND MUSHROOMS
Yield: Serves 6-8

Collards are divine and this recipe is a great alternative to boiling them to death with a ham hock. I promise you, most kids will even eat them this way. If collards season is over then use kale which you'll only need to parboil for half the time as the collards.

Ingredients:
2 large bunches collard greens, de-stemmed, cut into bite-size pieces and washed
2 tablespoons extra virgin olive oil
2 tablespoons coconut oil
½ lb. of shiitake mushrooms or Baby Bella's thinly sliced
½ head of garlic, minced
½ teaspoon sea salt
½ cup chicken broth
Salt and fresh ground pepper to taste

Procedure:
1. In a pot of boiling, salted water (like the sea), cook the cut collards in two batches for about 5-6 minutes, drain in a colander and quickly spread them out on a roasting pan so that they won't keep cooking on top of each other.
2. Heat a large sauté pan on medium heat. Add the olive oil, mushrooms & ¼ teaspoon of the sea salt and constantly stir until the mushrooms are seared and cooked through, about 5 minutes.
3. Remove the mushrooms to a side dish and add the coconut oil, garlic & ¼ teaspoon of the sea

salt to the pan and sauté until light brown for about 1-2 minutes.
4. Add in the blanched collards, mushrooms, chicken broth and sauté for about 5 minutes. Make sure that the collards have been well mixed with the garlic and mushrooms.
5. Season with fresh ground black pepper & salt and serve hot or at room temperature.

Notes:

--A great way to prepare hearty greens for the week is to parboil them for about 5-6 minutes first and then you can set them aside in the fridge until you need them for their second cooking. Parboiling also helps to make the heartier greens like collards and kale a little less chewy and bitter.

--You can use whatever type of mushrooms you want to for this recipe. Shitakes are lovely if you're having a dinner party and want to spend a little more money but Baby Bella's are just as tasty.

--To spice it up a bit, I sometimes add a heaping ¼ teaspoon of red pepper flakes in when I'm sautéing the garlic, but too spicy for children.

DEVILED TOMATOES

A new and fresh twist on "Deviled Eggs"
Yield: 6 servings

Ingredients:

6 small tomatoes or large Roma tomatoes, halved
    with the seeds and membrane removed
3 scallions, chopped using 2 inches of the light to dark
    green parts
½ green pepper, diced
½ large cucumber seeded and small diced
1 teaspoon of fresh squeezed lemon juice
1 heaping tablespoon of finely chopped Italian flat leaf
    parsley
1 heaping tablespoon of minced fresh dill
¼ teaspoon of sea salt
¾ cup plain Greek yogurt
Salt and fresh ground pepper to taste

Procedure:

1. Cut off a bit of the stem end of the tomatoes.
   Cut them in half and using a spoon scoop out
   the seeds and membrane of tomato and leave
   the flesh. Wipe and dry out each tomato half
   as much as you can with a paper towel and set
   aside.
2. In a medium bowl combine: scallions, green
   pepper, cucumber, lemon juice, parsley, dill,
   salt and yogurt and mix it all together well.
3. Add more salt, pepper and lemon juice to taste.

4. Take the mixture and fill each tomato until it's heaping with this yogurt, veggie goodness and top with a pretty little sprig of that fresh dill.

Uses:

- Depending on how big these tomato halves are you might want to serve them as a side dish to some barbecued chicken or as a main course on a hot summer day surrounded by a nice green salad and lemon vinaigrette.
- The yogurt mixture also makes a wonderful dip for raw veggies or chips and crackers of any kind.

BROCCOLI WITH MUSHROOMS & ROASTED RED PEPPERS

Yield: Serves 6-8

This is a wonderful savory side dish that will go well with just about anything. I want you to use up the rest of those roasted red peppers that you used for the hummus recipe last week. ☺

Ingredients:
2 tablespoons butter
2 tablespoons extra-virgin olive oil
3 cloves garlic, finely chopped
1 8oz. package sliced mushrooms
2 heads broccoli, using florets only, equaling 8 cups
    broccoli
½ cup chicken broth
½-3/4 teaspoon sea salt
Ground pepper
½ cup roasted jarred red peppers, rinsed, dried and
    coarsely chopped
Fresh grated parmesan Reggiano cheese

Procedure:
1. In a large sauté pan with fitted lid over medium heat melt the butter into the olive oil then add in the garlic and sauté for 1 minute, next add the mushrooms and cook for another 2 minutes. Add in the broccoli and broth, stirring well, place the lid on pan and simmer for 8-10 minutes stirring every few minutes.
2. When broccoli is just tender, but still crisp add the sea salt, pepper and roasted red peppers

and mix well, cook for another minute and serve.
3. Grate some fresh parmesan Reggiano cheese on top of each serving.

Notes:

The pan I love is stainless steel by Calphalon, 5 quart and 12" wide...I use it all the time!

SWEET AND SOUR COLESLAW

Yield: Serves 6-8

Ingredients:

4 cups (packed) thinly sliced/shredded white cabbage
1 cup (packed) thinly sliced/shredded red cabbage
1 medium Vidalia sweet onion, thinly sliced
1 cup grated carrots
1 tablespoon honey
3 tablespoons apple cider vinegar
1 tablespoon Dijon mustard
½ teaspoon celery seeds
¾ teaspoon of sea salt
¼ cup extra-virgin olive oil
1/8 teaspoon ground pepper to taste
¼ cup toasted sunflower seeds

Procedure:

1. In a medium bowl place the cabbages, onion and carrots and toss well.
2. In a small bowl whisk together the honey, vinegar, mustard, celery seeds, sea salt, olive oil, and pepper.
3. Once the mixture boils then remove from the heat and whisk in the oil.
4. While the liquid is still hot, pour it over the vegetables and mix well. Salt and pepper to taste.
5. You can cover and refrigerate it overnight or serve at room temperature and crunchy...both ways are delicious.
6. Just be sure to toss it well before serving and season with more salt and pepper if necessary

and sprinkle toasted sunflower seeds over the top just before serving.

GRILLED ROSEMARY SQUASH

Yield: Serves 4-6

When yellow "crook neck" squash is in season it is so sweet and delicious and grilling it just brings out all of its sweetness.

Ingredients:
3 tablespoons extra-virgin olive oil
1 tablespoon fresh rosemary, finely chopped
1 teaspoon, sea salt
½ teaspoon fresh ground black pepper
5 medium yellow "crook neck" squash, cut into ½ inch vertical slices

Procedure:
1. Toss all the ingredients in a big bowl until all the squash slices are well coated with the rosemary, olive oil, salt and pepper.
2. On a "hot" grill lay the squash on one side for about 3 minutes, flip it over and grill it for another 2 minutes. Serve it hot off the grill or at room temperature.

SUGAR SNAP PEAS & RED PEPPERS

Yield: 6 servings

This is a crispy and delightful side veggie dish that I'm suggesting you serve with the "Coconut Shrimp Pasta." Make sure you don't cook the veggies too long because you want them to keep a bit of their crisp.

Ingredients:

¾ lb. (about 3 cups) fresh sugar snap peas, ends removed & cut in half
2 small red bell peppers sliced, ¼" thick and cut in half (about 2 cups)
1 ½ tablespoon extra-virgin olive oil
1 tablespoon soy sauce
1 tablespoon toasted sesame oil
1 ½ teaspoons sesame seeds
1/8 teaspoon sea salt and ground pepper

Procedure:

1. Heat olive oil in a 12" sauté pan over medium heat. Add in snap peas & red bell pepper, sauté for 4-5 minutes.
2. Place the veggies in a serving bowl and pour the soy sauce, toasted sesame oil, sesame seeds, salt, pepper and toss to coat and serve.

EGGPLANT PARMESAN

Yield: Serves 4

This is a tasty and satisfying Eggplant Parm because we didn't fry the eggplant we browned it under the broiler. This is one of my recipes that we taped for an episode of "Don't Tell Mama" on KitchenDaily.com. So if you want to "see" how this dish is made then just tune in online!

Ingredients:
2 tablespoons extra-virgin olive oil, plus additional for brushing pans
2 pounds eggplant, trimmed and sliced lengthwise into ¼ inch thick slices
2 cups whole milk ricotta
4 tablespoons finely grated fresh Parmesan
1 large egg, beaten
1 garlic clove, minced
½ teaspoon each sea salt and pepper
14 large or 28 small fresh basil leaves
2 cups store-bought "organic" marinara sauce

Procedure:
1. Slice the eggplant into long strips, chopping off the stem and cutting off the fleshy sides as they will be too thick to roll. Preheat broiler and lightly oil 2 large sheet pans. Brush slices of eggplant with olive oil on both sides, then arrange in one layer on the bottom of each pan. Broil eggplant in batches, turning once, until golden brown on both sides, about 2 minutes per side. Let cool.

2. Preheat oven to 375°F. Spoon 1 cup of marinara sauce in bottom of an 8-inch square baking dish.
3. Add ricotta to a bowl for mixing. Beat one large egg and add to the ricotta. Add 2 tablespoons Parmesan, garlic, and salt and pepper. Whisk ingredients until well-mixed.
4. Arrange a basil leaf on each slice of eggplant and top with 2 tablespoons of ricotta filling, spreading it evenly down the eggplant. Starting at a short end, roll up eggplant and arrange seam side down in prepared baking dish. Repeat with remaining eggplant, basil, and ricotta filling and arrange in one layer in dish. Spoon ½ cup more sauce over top of eggplant and sprinkle with remaining 2 tablespoons Parmesan.
5. Bake, uncovered in middle of oven, until sauce is bubbling and heated through, 25 to 30 minutes. Serve with remaining ½ cup sauce on side.

MEAT AND POULTRY

SPICY-ROASTED CHICKEN AND SWEET POTATOES
Yield: Serves 6-8

Talk about comfort food...roast chicken and sweet potatoes, yum! Easy, too! My husband, Alex and I like food with a little zipparooni, but if you have young ones and they don't like the spice then just cut down on the cayenne or don't use it at all.

Ingredients:
3 tablespoons extra-virgin olive oil
1 ½ tablespoons paprika
1 teaspoon ground cumin
½ teaspoon cinnamon
½ teaspoon cayenne
2 teaspoon sea salt
1 teaspoon ground pepper
1 whole chicken (about 3 ½ - 4lb) buy it cut up or do it yourself!
2 medium-sized sweet potatoes cut into ½ inch moons, with or without skin
1 onion cut into ½ inch slices

Procedure:
1. Place the oven rack in the upper third of the oven.
2. Preheat oven to 500°F
3. In small bowl mix together paprika, cumin, cinnamon, cayenne, salt and pepper.

4. In a large bowl put the onion and potatoes in first then add in the chicken. Pour the olive oil over the chicken and then evenly distribute the spice mixture all over the chicken and veggies. Mix all of the ingredients well so that everything has a nice coating of spice and oil. (Use your hands, it's a lot easier.)
5. Pour all the ingredients onto a shallow baking pan and arrange all the chicken pieces skin-side up and resting on top of the onion and potatoes.
6. Bake until the chicken is just cooked through about 30-35 minutes. Be sure to drizzle any pan juices onto the chicken when serving.

Notes:

Focus on buying chickens that are raised without antibiotics and hormones. If you don't know how to cut a whole chicken up...now is the time to empower yourself! Go to www.gourmet.com and do a search on "how to cut up a chicken" and voila you'll watch the video and do it yourself. Chicken is less expensive when bought whole or you can just buy it already cut up and carry on. If there is any leftover chicken then reserve it for the "Roasted Chicken and Cheese Quesadillas" you'll make in a few nights!

ROASTED CHICKEN AND CHEESE QUESADILLAS
Yield: Serves 4

I don't know anyone who doesn't love a little cheesy quesadilla. Fun food can also be nutritious food. Roast enough chicken earlier in the week to create leftovers. Come Soup night cook up some of these quesadillas and your meal is complete and satisfying. But, a lovely little side salad would be a welcome addition.

Ingredients:
8 small corn or 4 10-inch whole wheat tortillas
1 cup grated cheddar or jack cheese or both
½ teaspoon smoked paprika*
½ teaspoon sea salt
1 cup shredded leftover chicken or 8 slices deli turkey
 meat
Fresh or jarred salsa

Procedure:
1. Heat a 12 inch skillet over medium heat and place two of the tortillas in the skillet to heat up for about a minute. If using the larger tortilla then heat it up and pull half of it up on the side of the pan so that only half of each tortilla is lying on the bottom of the pan. On each tortilla half sprinkle ¼ cup of the cheese, a good pinch of smoked paprika and a good pinch of sea salt in that order. Then lay ¼ cup of the chicken or deli meat on top of the cheese and fold over the other half of the larger tortilla or place

another small tortilla on top of the chicken making a sandwich.
2. Cook over medium heat for 2 minutes, flip and cook another 2 minutes on the other side. Serve it up with a little side of salsa.

Notes:

--McCormick Spices makes the Smoked Paprika sold in grocery stores. A little goes a long way and it is a divine addition to everything from dips to quesadillas, spice rubs, rice dishes, soups, etc.

--A note about tortillas: just read the ingredients of any package before you buy it and make sure you understand what all the ingredients are. It's a crying shame that we have to be such detectives about our food but, if you didn't make it from real ingredients in your own kitchen I guarantee you the food will have some less-than-desirable ingredients in it. So, just keep it real, honey!

HERBED MEATLOAF

Yield: Serves 6-8

Using the fresh herbs of spring and summer you can really create a flavorful meatloaf along with a few other delicious ingredients. Mix this meatloaf up the night before and then just bring it to room temperature for about 15 minutes, ice with your ketchup mixture and bake for an hour with some roasted Yukon gold potatoes. A side of greens and that's dinner. Not to mention a good meatloaf sandwich for any takers. ☺

Ingredients:
3 tbsp. bacon fat or extra-virgin olive oil
3 cloves garlic, minced
1 tablespoon + 1 teaspoon chopped fresh thyme or 2
    teaspoons dried thyme
½ large onion, small diced, about one cup
1 medium carrot, small diced, about ½ cup
2 lbs. grass-fed ground beef*
1 heaping cup cooked quinoa
1 egg, beaten
1 ½ teaspoon sea salt
½ teaspoon ground pepper
¼ cup finely chopped flat leaf, "Italian" parsley
½ cup organic ketchup
2 tablespoons Chipotle Tobasco Sauce**

Procedure:
1. Preheat oven to 350°F, placing the oven rack in the middle.
2. In a 12" skillet over medium heat melt the bacon fat and add in the garlic, thyme, onion and carrot and sauté for 5 minutes. Take off

the heat and let cool while mixing together the rest of the meatloaf ingredients.

3. In a large bowl add the ground beef, quinoa, egg, salt, pepper and parsley. And, once the cooked veggie mixture has cooled for at least 5 minutes then add it in as well. Using your hands thoroughly mix all ingredients well.
4. Using a standard loaf pan press the meatloaf into the pan with a bit of a rounded top.
5. Mix together the ketchup and Chipotle Tobasco and spread/ice the raw meatloaf with the ketchup mixture. And, if you like that combo then you may have to make some more to serve at the table with the meatloaf.
6. Bake the meatloaf for an hour or until the internal temperature of the meatloaf reaches 145°F. After cooking let the meatloaf rest, covered for five minutes then serve.

Notes:

*Grass-fed beef – Visit your local farmers market and you will most certainly find grass-fed beef from a local farmer and you can find it at most local grocery stores as well. Grass-fed beef is really lean and high in omega-3's because of all the green grass the cows eat…good for them and good for us!

**Chipotle Tobasco – you can find this in your local grocery store next to the regular Tobasco sauce. I love this stuff and add it to many a food item. It has heat but it's very flavorful.

CHICKEN SAUSAGE AND PEPPERS

Yield: Serves 6-8

This dish comes together in no time and is also great with lamb sausage if that's available at your local farmer's market in the spring. So, with the savory flavor of the chicken sausage the peppers add a nice sweetness to the dish. This is perfect with brown rice or quinoa as a side.

Ingredients:

2 tablespoons extra-virgin olive oil
1 medium red bell pepper cut into ¼" slices
1 medium green bell pepper cut into ¼" slices
1 medium onion cut into ¼" sauté slices
3 cloves garlic, coarsely chopped
½ teaspoon dried oregano
½ teaspoon dried thyme
¼ teaspoon sea salt
Fresh cracked pepper
2 -1 lb. packages cooked chicken sausage

Procedure:

1. In a large skillet over medium heat sauté the olive oil, peppers, onion, herbs and salt until they just soften, about 5 minutes.
2. Remove the vegetable mixture from the pan and set it aside.
3. Add the chicken sausage to the skillet over medium heat and brown the sausage for about 2-3 minutes on each side. Add a little more olive oil to the pan if need be.

4. Add the vegetables back into the pan.
5. Place a lid on the pot and simmer over medium-low for 5 minutes and serve.

Notes: Don't forget you probably can find all kinds of wonderful sausages from your local farmers. Just remember they'll probably be raw and you just need to cook the sausage longer. Knowing where your meat comes from and how the animals are treated really does bring peace of mind at the end of the day.

ROSEMARY-LEMON ROASTED CHICKEN WITH NEW POTATOES & CARROTS

Yield: Serves 6-8

Roasted chicken in any variety is a staple in my diet nearly every week year round because you can do so much with leftover roasted chicken…if there are any leftovers. What's not to love about rosemary and lemon…that speaks spring/summer to me along with some new potatoes and farm-fresh sweet carrots.

Ingredients:
2 tablespoons butter, melted
2 tablespoons extra-virgin olive oil
1 ½ tablespoons finely chopped fresh rosemary
1 ½ tablespoons fresh lemon juice
2 teaspoons sea salt
1 teaspoon ground pepper
1 whole chicken (about 3 ½ - 4 ½ lbs) buy it cut up or do it yourself!
2 lbs. small-medium new potatoes (about 10-12), skin on, quartered
1 lb. carrots quartered 3" long wedges

Procedure for cooking the fish:
1. Place the oven rack in the upper third of the oven
2. Preheat oven to 500℉
3. In small bowl mix together butter, olive oil, rosemary, lemon juice, salt and pepper, set aside.
4. In a large bowl put the potatoes and carrots in first then add in the cut up chicken. Pour the

rosemary mixture over the chicken. Mix all of the ingredients well so that everything has a nice herb coating. (Use your hands, it's a lot easier.) ☺

5.   Pour all the ingredients onto a shallow baking pan and arrange all the chicken pieces skin-side up and resting on top of the potatoes and carrots.

6.   Bake until the chicken is just cooked through about 30-35 minutes. Remove just the chicken to a platter and loosely cover with foil. Continue roasting the carrots and potatoes for another 10 minutes. Pour the veggies and juices over the chicken and serve family style.

Notes:

Try buying your chicken from a local farmer or at the farmer's market and make sure it has been raised without hormones and antibiotics at a minimum. You can also find "healthy chickens" in most local grocery stores now, too. So if you don't know how to cut a whole chicken up…now is the time to empower yourself! Go to www.gourmet.com and do a search on "how to cut up a chicken" and voila you'll watch the video and do it yourself. Chicken is cheaper when bought whole or you can just buy it already cut up and carry on. If there is any leftover chicken then reserve it for the "Roasted Chicken and Cheese Quesadillas" you'll make in several nights!

PEAS AND RICE (with Kielbasa to boot!)

Yield: Serves 6-8

I spent the majority of my childhood growing up in the Bahamas and what a blessing that was. One of the things I loved most about living in the islands was the Bahamian food, all that fresh seafood and especially the "peas and rice." So, this recipe is my grown-up healthy American take on "Peas and Rice" and I've added some extra protein in the form of turkey kielbasa so this is meant to be a main-course dish. You can use whatever kind of peas you'd like, but since there are so many fresh peas in season in the summer, I've used the Purple Hull's and they are delicious, but the Crowder Peas are really delicious too. But if you're in a hurry feel free to use frozen, but cook them or canned black eyed peas.

Ingredients:

4 cups **cooked** long-grain brown rice (leftover from
    Day 2 Salmon Dinner)
2 cups fresh Purple Hull Peas or frozen Black Eyed
    Peas
3 cups of chicken broth
2 tablespoons extra virgin olive oil
1 tablespoon butter
3 cloves garlic, minced
2 cups onion, finely chopped
1 cup carrot, cut into ¼ inch pieces
½ pound turkey kielbasa cut into ¼" pieces*
1 ½ tablespoons fresh thyme, chopped or 2
    teaspoons dried thyme
¾ teaspoon sea salt
3 tablespoons coarsely chopped flat-leaf parsley
Sea Salt and fresh ground pepper to taste

Procedure:
1. Cook the peas in 3 cups of chicken broth simmering on a low boil for about 30-40 minutes or until they are just done. Set them aside. This can be done earlier in the day or the night before.
2. Using a large sauté pan over medium heat add the olive oil, butter, garlic, onion, carrot, ¼ tsp. of sea salt and sauté for about 3-5 minutes or until the onion is translucent.
3. Add the kielbasa and thyme to the vegetables and cook for another 2 minutes.
4. Using a slotted spoon, leaving the broth behind dish the peas along with the cooked rice and ½ teaspoon of sea salt into the sauté pan with the sautéed veggies. Mix everything together so that all the ingredients are evenly distributed throughout the dish.
5. Add more salt and pepper to taste and continue to sauté until everything is completely heated through, 5-10 minutes and serve.

*Kielbasa can be found in the cooler with the hot dogs at your local grocery store. Just remember, no nitrates or nitrites please. It is smoked and usually pre-cooked but you want to make sure it's heated well so that all its great flavor comes alive.

SEAFOOD

SALMON WITH LEMON-DILL BUTTER
Yield: Serves 4-6

Eating wild-caught Alaskan salmon at least once, if not twice a week is a great idea. Wild salmon is high in the essential fatty acid Omega-3 which has anti-inflammatory benefits for our brains and bodies and we could all use some anti-inflammation in our lives these days. This is just a very simple and quick way of preparing a very healthful food.

Ingredients:
4 five-six ounce salmon filets with skin-on or off
1 tbsp. Extra-virgin olive oil
¼ tsp. sea salt
1/8 teaspoon ground pepper

Lemon-Dill Butter:
1 stick butter
2 cloves garlic finely chopped
1 tablespoon fresh lemon juice
2 tablespoon finely chopped fresh dill or 1 tablespoon dried dill
¼ teaspoon sea salt
¼ teaspoon ground pepper

Procedure:
1. Preheat oven to 425°F and place rack in the upper third of oven.
2. In a small saucepan over medium-low heat combine butter, garlic, lemon juice, dill, sea salt

and pepper, simmer for two minutes and set to the side.
3. Wash each filet in cold water and pat dry with paper towel. Line a baking sheet with parchment paper. Brush the under sides of the fish with the olive oil and place skin-side down, if it has skin. Drizzle 1 tablespoon of the butter sauce on each filet. Sprinkle with sea salt and pepper. Bake for 10-12 minutes until opaque/just cooked through.
4. Let fish rest for a minute while you reheat the lemon-dill butter sauce and spoon it over a serving of fish, garnish with a thin slice of lemon, fresh sprig of dill and put the rest on the table for a little extra yummy drizzle.

Notes:

There will be extra butter sauce left over so just put it in the fridge and sauté some delicious yellow squash with it later in the week.

MEDITERRANEAN FISH CASSEROLE
Yield: Serves 4-6

I love Mediterranean flavors of any kind and this fish dish definitely comes through on being light and flavorful at the same time. This is a good one to serve up on a hot summer night. I want to thank my dear friend Jenny for sharing this wonderful recipe with me…she cooked it for us once and I just loved it. I made a few changes to it but the premise is the same…yumminess!

Ingredients:
2 large bell peppers – red, green or yellow, thinly sliced, the long way
2 medium-sized fennel bulbs thinly sliced after removing the stems and root end
2 tablespoons extra-virgin olive oil
¼ teaspoon sea salt
1/8 teaspoon ground pepper

Tomato/Olive Mixture to Top Fish:
4 cloves garlic, coarsely chopped
2 cups cherry tomatoes, quartered
½ cup pitted Kalamata olives, chopped
½ cup chopped flat-leaf parsley
2 tablespoons lemon juice
2 tablespoons extra-virgin olive oil
¼ - ½ teaspoon sea salt, taste before adding more
¼ teaspoon ground pepper
4 – ¾ inch thick cod or halibut filets

Procedure:
1. Preheat oven to 400°F and place rack in the middle of the oven.
2. In a large casserole pan toss the peppers, fennel, olive oil, salt and pepper until everything is well coated and roast in the oven for 25 minutes.
3. Meanwhile, in a medium bowl mix together garlic, tomatoes, olives, parsley, lemon juice, olive oil, salt and pepper.
4. After the peppers and fennel finish cooking remove pan from oven and stir all the veggies and spread out evenly. Season the fish filets with a bit of salt and pepper and place them across the veggies and spoon all of the tomato/olive mixture all over the tops of the filets. Bake for another 15 minutes until the fish flakes apart and serve.

SALMON WITH CREAMY HERB SAUCE/DRESSING

Yield: Serves 4-6

Salmon is a great and super healthy base for lots of sauces. Since we have so many herbs to choose from in spring and summer I decided to add a few into this delicious and creamy sauce which can also be used as a salad dressing!

Ingredients:
4 five-six ounce salmon filets with skin-on or off
1 tbsp. Extra-virgin olive oil
¼ tsp. sea salt
Ground pepper

Creamy Herb Sauce/Dressing:
1 tablespoon flax seed oil
½ cup plain Greek yogurt
¼ cup full-fat sour cream
3 tablespoons chopped fresh chives
2 tablespoons chopped fresh parsley
1 ½ tablespoons capers, rinsed*
1 teaspoon fresh lemon juice
¼ teaspoon sea salt
1/8 teaspoon ground pepper

Procedure:
1. Preheat oven to 425℉ and place rack in the upper third of oven.
2. In a blender or food processor combine all the ingredients for the Creamy Herb Sauce and

pulse until just combined and set aside. This will be served at room temperature.
3. Wash each filet in cold water and pat dry with paper towel. Line a baking sheet with parchment paper. Brush the under sides of the fish with the olive oil and place skin-side down, if it has skin.   Sprinkle with ¼ teaspoon sea salt and pepper. Bake for 10-12 minutes until opaque/just cooked through.
4. Plate the fish and pour a tablespoon or two of the Creamy Herb Sauce over the top.

Notes:

Any leftover sauce/dressing? Use it on your salad one day.

*Capers can be found in the jarred pickle aisle of your grocery store. They need to be rinsed because they have been preserved in salty brine.

COCONUT SHRIMP SOUP with NOODLES
Yield: Serves 4-6

Shrimp is America's favorite seafood so I thought I'd give this Thai flavored dish a little Italian leaning and serve it over a bit of pasta. This is a night that I encourage you to take a break and go out to eat, but if you don't then you'll at least have something yummy to make!

Ingredients:
1 can full-fat coconut milk*
½ cup water
2 tablespoons Thai Kitchen Premium Fish Sauce*
1/3 cup fresh lime juice
1" piece of fresh ginger, sliced and bruised
2 tablespoons maple syrup
1 medium carrot cut in half and sliced ¼" thick
2 tablespoons Thai Kitchen Roasted Red Chili Paste*
¼ cup thinly sliced on diagonal scallions/spring onions
1 ¼ lbs. wild-caught shrimp, shelled and de-veined**
3 tablespoons chopped fresh cilantro leaves

Pasta: Whole grain angel hair pasta boiled in well-salted water for about 6 minutes, ½ cup serving in the bottom of each bowl. Or if you have gluten issues then boil up some Buckwheat Udon noodles, delicious. You can find these in the Asian section of the grocery store along with the fish sauce and chili paste.

Procedure:
1. In a 3 quart sauce/soup pan bring to a boil over high heat coconut milk, water, fish sauce, lime

juice, ginger, maple syrup and carrot. Simmer this mixture for 10 minutes.
2. Meanwhile start the water boiling for the pasta...get that cooked, drained and set aside.
3. Removing ½ cup of coconut liquid into a bowl mix in the 2 tablespoons of roasted red chili paste and whisk until there are no more lumps and add back into the pan.
4. Bring the "coconut milk sauce" to a boil, add in the scallions and shrimp and cook for 3-4 minutes. Remove the piece of fresh ginger. Serve a ladle of shrimp and coconut milk over pasta in a bowl and garnish with a couple of teaspoons of chopped cilantro leaves.

Notes:

*You can find the coconut milk, fish sauce and chili paste in the Thai/international section of the grocery store. If not, then try the local health food store.

**You may find wild-caught shrimp in your grocery store's seafood freezer section or it might be fresh at the seafood counter and then you'll probably have to shell and de-vein them...lots of work, but worth it! If the shrimp do have the shell on, then buy 1 ½ lbs. of shrimp.

SNACKS

ROASTED RED PEPPER HUMMUS
Yield: Serves 10-15 for a snack

Who doesn't love hummus? It's a healthful snack food because the chick peas are given a great boost in vitamin C and lycopene with the addition of roasted red peppers. Hummus is great as a spread on sandwiches as well as for dipping pita chips and veggies. I use a food processor for this recipe because it makes life oh so much easier.

Ingredients:
2 cloves of garlic, finely chopped or use a garlic press for a stronger garlic flavor
2 15oz. cans of garbanzo beans/chickpeas, rinsed and drained well
1/3 cup Tahini*
1 teaspoon ground cumin
¼ cup fresh lemon juice
3 tablespoon virgin olive oil
1 tablespoon flax seed oil
¾ cup roasted red peppers, washed and dried**
½ teaspoon and a few good pinches sea salt
1/8 teaspoon ground pepper
1-2 tablespoon water, if needed to thin the hummus

Procedure:
Add everything except the water into the bowl of the food processor and turn it on stopping occasionally to scrape down the sides. Continue to process the hummus until the mixture is completely smooth about

4-5 minutes total. Add in the water one teaspoon at a time if needed to thin out the hummus.

Notes:
I want to encourage you to buy a food processor if you don't have one because there are a million and one ways you can use it to speed up many a process in your kitchen. And if you have one that's been collecting dust on the shelf…then I challenge you to get it out and try it with this recipe.

When serving, sprinkle a little smoked paprika and drizzle a little more EVOO on top. McCormick Spices makes a smoked paprika and it is divine!

*Tahini is just sesame seed paste that is used often in middle eastern cooking and can be found at any grocery store in the ethnic section.

**Roasted Red Peppers can be found in any grocery store in the "pickle" area. They should be packed in a glass jar with the following ingredients: peppers, water, salt and citric acid…that's it. They are a great addition to a lot of vegetable side dishes.

GRANOLA BARS

Yield: Serves about 16 for a snack

I know that a lot of kids like granola for snacks and cereal and in a yogurt parfait after school and so I had to try my hand at my own "healthy" version of a granola bar. I used oat flour since I have a difficult time digesting wheat, but you can certainly use whole-wheat flour in this recipe. Just remember to serve a nice chilled glass of whole milk with your granola bar...satisfaction guaranteed!

Ingredients:
1 cup rolled oats
1 cup sliced almonds
1 cup shredded unsweetened/desiccated coconut*
½ cup raw sunflower seeds
¼ cup coconut oil** melted & extra to grease baking dish
2/3 cup pure maple syrup
1 teaspoon cinnamon
1 ½ teaspoon vanilla extract
¼ teaspoon sea salt
½ cup almond butter or peanut butter
1 cup oat or whole-wheat flour
½ cup raisins
½ cup dried cranberries, cherries or blueberries

Procedure:
1. Preheat oven to 350°F.
2. On a baking sheet mix together the oats, almonds, coconut and sunflower seeds and toast in the oven for 10 minutes, stirring once

until lightly browned. Then set aside and let cool. Lower the oven temperature to 300℉.
3. Meanwhile, in a small sauce pan over medium-high heat whisk together coconut oil, maple syrup, cinnamon, vanilla extract, sea salt and almond/peanut butter. Bring mixture to a boil and then simmer for a few minutes and remove pan from the heat.
4. In a large bowl mix together the dried fruits and oat flour. Then add in the oats, almonds, coconut and sunflower seeds and then the liquid ingredients and stir well until every part of the mixture is moist.
5. In a greased 8"x12" baking dish, line the bottom with parchment paper.
6. Pour the granola mixture in and press down until it is evenly distributed across the bottom of the pan.
7. Bake for 25-30 minutes until light golden brown.
8. Let cool for an hour and then cut into 2" x 3" rectangular bars. Let cool completely and then store in an airtight container for several days…if they last that long.

Notes:

*Shredded/desiccated unsweetened coconut is just coconut "meat" that has been grated and dehydrated to remove all the moisture and has no added sweetener. You might be able to find this in the health food section of your grocery store or just head to your local health food store. You can buy incredible coconut products online at: www.tropicaltraditions.com and www.vitacost.com

**Coconut Oil –This marvelous oil has gotten such a bad rap in recent history because it's almost completely saturated. But, you have to understand that this saturated fat is so good for us in many ways: it has anti-viral, anti-fungal and anti-bacterial properties because it has lauric acid which is in breast milk and boosts your immune system. It's the type of fat that is used by top athletes and people who want to lose weight because half of it is burned for energy by the body. Coconut oil is also excellent in helping to support brain function and who doesn't need that now days?

Where to get coconut oil? Some grocery stores might have it in the health food section, but otherwise you need to go to a health food store or order it online at a lower cost. Here's the important part…you want to buy "virgin-unrefined" coconut oil so that it's not highly processed or hydrogenated by the time you get it. So, just read the label carefully.

CHEESY POPCORN

Yield: Serves 4-6 for a snack

Move over Cheetos and store-bought cheese popcorn…there is a new more delicious and good for you cheese popcorn in town. This is a great pick me up in the afternoon for you and your family or to bag and take with you to the movie theater. I promise, you'll never want to microwave your popcorn again after eating this!

Ingredients:
2 tablespoons unrefined/virgin coconut oil*
¼ cup + 3 tablespoons "organic" popping corn kernels
¼ cup finely grated parmesan cheese (the powdery kind)
4 tablespoons butter melted
Sea salt to taste

Procedure:
1. Melt the coconut oil over medium-high heat, add corn kernels and put the lid on the pan. When you hear the first kernel pop then turn the heat down just a bit and start sliding the pan back and forth on the burner until you hear the popping slow way down and almost stop, then remove it from the heat.
2. Pour popcorn into a big mixing bowl, sprinkle cheese evenly over top.
3. Melt the butter and drizzle all over the popcorn, then toss with your hands, taste and decide if you need a little sea salt to finish it.

Notes:
*Coconut Oil –This marvelous oil has gotten such a bad rap in recent history because it's almost completely saturated. But, you have to understand that this saturated fat is so good for us in so many ways like: it has anti-viral, anti-fungal and anti-bacterial properties because it has lauric acid which you can find in breast milk. It's the type of fat that is used by top athletes and people who want to lose weight because half of it is always used for energy by the body. I could go on and on about its benefits but, why don't you do the research and see if there are any scientific studies out there showing you what's so bad about coconut oil. More on all this subject later.

Where to get coconut oil? Some grocery stores might have it in the health food section, but otherwise you need to go to a health food store or order online. Here's the important part…you want to buy "virgin" coconut oil so that it's not highly processed by the time you get it. So, just read the label carefully.

SMOKED SALMON DILL DIP
Yield: 2 ½ - 3 cups

Who doesn't love a good dip that's satisfying and good for you? This is just another great snack idea for kids after school or if you're making a wrap for their lunch then spread a little of this on their wrap or sandwich. It's just another yummy way to get some of the goodness of salmon in our diets.

Ingredients:
8 ounces full-fat cream cheese (organic, if possible)
½ cup plain Greek yogurt
¼ cup coarsely chopped fresh dill
4 ounce package smoked salmon*
1 teaspoon fresh lemon juice
1/8 tsp. sea salt

Procedure:
Combine all the ingredients into the bowl of a food processor. Puree the mixture for 2-3 minutes stopping every 30 seconds to scrape down the sides. Spoon it into a glass/ceramic container and store in the fridge for 5-6 days. Serve it up with celery sticks and/or whole-wheat pita chips, with the least ingredients.

Notes:
*You can find smoked salmon in the refrigerator compartment next to the seafood counter or freezer section in your grocer.

"ALMOND JOY" COOKIES

Yield: 26 cookies

I can resist most "sweet treats" unless they include two things...coconut and chocolate. Whenever I was allowed a candy bar as a kid I always wanted an Almond Joy so, I decided to come up with a yummy and healthy version. I use a lot less sugar and unsweetened coconut. This also qualifies as a great gluten-free treat, too.

Ingredients:
1 cup whole raw almonds
1 tablespoon pure maple syrup
4 egg whites*
½ teaspoon sea salt
½ cup Sucanat/Rapadura (organic whole can sugar)**
½ teaspoon vanilla extract
½ cup unsweetened cocoa powder
1 ½ cups shredded, unsweetened coconut

Procedure:

1. Place one oven rack in the upper third of oven and second rack in lower third of oven.
2. Preheat the oven to 325°F and place parchment paper on two baking sheets.
3. Using a small bowl, mix together almonds and maple syrup until all nuts are coated, set aside.
4. Beat egg whites and salt until soft peaks form, slowly beat in sucanat until stiffer peaks form, then beat in vanilla and cocoa powder, be prepared because the egg whites will flatten

now. These steps will take about 2 minutes. Stir in the coconut until well mixed.
5. Measure tablespoon drops of batter onto the parchment. Press one almond in the middle of each cookie. Spread remaining almonds around the cookie sheet where there is room because you will bake the almonds at the same time as the cookies. Bake for 10 minutes and switch the cookie sheets to the other rack and then bake for another 10 minutes, let cool and pour a glass of milk! Serve the extra almonds with the cookies for some added goodness.

Notes:

*Don't waist those egg yolks, go ahead and blend a smoothie and put it in the fridge as a snack for later or the next morning. Just make sure your eggs are fresh from a local farmer.

**Sucanat or Rapadura (sugar cane natural) or "organic whole cane sugar" as the package now says is what sucanat is. It is sugar cane juice with all of its goodness and minerals intact that has been dehydrated and grated. You can always use sucanat in equal measure to refined sugar. The difference is in the taste and sucanat tastes and is less sweet than white sugar and you just "feel better" after eating a sweet treat made with sucanat/whole cane sugar. Some grocery stores are carrying this in their "health food section" otherwise, you'll find it at your local health food store. It's really worth the trip!

GRAINS

BROWN RICE
Yield: Serves 6-8

Brown rice can be a little challenging to make if you're not in the routine of cooking it. So, like oatmeal and grits it is best to soak this grain in room temperature water with a little apple cider vinegar or lemon juice for about 24 hours to start to break it down so that it is easier to digest, more delicious and will lessen the cooking time.

Ingredients:
1 cup long-grain brown rice
1 tablespoon apple cider vinegar or lemon juice
2 cups water for soaking
2 cups chicken or vegetable broth for cooking
1 teaspoon sea salt
2 tablespoons butter

Procedure:
1. In a hand-held mesh strainer thoroughly rinse the brown rice, place in a glass or ceramic bowl, add in apple cider vinegar or lemon juice, water, stir and cover. Leave on the countertop for 12-24 hours.
2. Strain the soaking water from the brown rice, place rice in a medium-sized sauce pan, add 2 cups of chicken or vegetable broth, salt and butter, bring to a boil, remove any "scum" from the surface, cover and reduce heat to a simmer and cook for about 40 minutes until all the liquid has evaporated. Leave the lid on and set

the rice aside to rest for 5 minutes to finish steaming.

Note:

I almost always make a double batch (2 cups raw grain) of brown rice because then I have it in the fridge for the next 4-5 days to serve as a part of any meal, like my "Crowder Peas, Brown Rice and Turkey Kielbasa Saute."

SALAD DRESSINGS

RANCH DRESSING
Yield: 1 1/3 cup

I am amazed at how much children love the store-bought "ranch" dressing. So I think my recipe comes pretty close to what's in the store except it's just made with nothing but real stuff. I mean, have you really looked at the ingredients in the store-bought variety? I honestly don't know what more than half of those chemicals are. So, just keep it real, honey and make your own...plus it's cheaper!

Ingredients:
1 medium garlic clove, minced
¾ cup full-fat Greek yogurt
½ cup buttermilk
2 small scallions, minced
2 teaspoons minced fresh dill or 1 teaspoon dried dill
1 ½ teaspoon apple cider vinegar
½ teaspoon sea salt & a few pinches
1/8 teaspoon ground black pepper

Procedure:
Just whisk everything together in a bowl and then transfer to a glass jar and it will keep in the fridge for a week if you used fresh ingredients in this recipe.

Notes:
Double the recipe especially if you have big "ranch" eaters...as most households do.
If you want to thicken this dressing then just add some real sour cream.

HONEY BALSAMIC VINAIGRETTE

Yield: About ¾ cup

I love a good balsamic vinaigrette and this has just a little more of the sweet and tangy thing going on. Come to think of it, this might make a good marinade for poultry...give it a try and let me know.

Ingredients:
1 tablespoon honey
¼ cup balsamic vinegar
1 tablespoon Dijon mustard
1 garlic clove squeezed through the garlic press
¼ cup + 3 tablespoons virgin olive oil
1 tablespoon flax seed oil
½ teaspoon sea salt
Ground pepper

Procedure:
In a small bowl whisk together the honey, vinegar, mustard and garlic until the honey is dissolved. Now slowly whisk in the oils until you see the dressing thicken. Finally, whisk in the salt and pepper. Dip a salad leaf into the dressing to taste it and make sure it will hold up on a salad.

Store the dressing in a glass jar and just shake well each time before using.

Notes:
It's important to know that when you make homemade salad dressing and taste it, by itself it should have a very strong flavor because the dressing will become

diluted as it thinly coats all the vegetables in your salad.

STRAWBERRY DRESSING
Yield: About 1 ¼ cup

A fruit dressing is a nice change from just a plain old vinaigrette sometimes…it's great on greens and you can get really wild and put it on some fresh strawberries or other fruit if you like!

Ingredients:
¼ cup white balsamic vinegar
¾ cup extra-virgin olive oil
½ cup chopped strawberries
1 tablespoon honey
¾ teaspoon sea salt
1/8 teaspoon ground pepper

Procedure:
1. Combine all ingredients in a blender or mini-food processor and puree until smooth and serve it…that's it.

SOUPS

TOMATO-BASIL SOUP WITH COCONUT MILK

Yield: 4 Servings

Alex loves a good tomato soup and I love to please my man! It's so easy to make and it's loaded full of goodness. If in season be sure to use some of that yummy fresh "summer" basil.

Ingredients:
1 tablespoon butter
1 tablespoon extra-virgin olive oil
2 cloves garlic, coarsely chopped
½ large yellow onion, small chopped
1 medium carrot, small diced
2 cups chicken stock
1 28 oz can diced tomatoes
½ cup coconut milk with no added sugar*
1 teaspoon dried basil or 1 tablespoon fresh-chopped
    basil
¼ teaspoon sea salt and more to taste
Ground pepper

Procedure:
1. In a 2 quart sauce pan over medium heat melt the butter into the olive oil and add in the garlic, onion and carrot and sauté for 3-4 minutes until the onion is translucent.
2. Add in the stock, tomatoes and dried basil if you're not using fresh and bring to a boil. Then bring the heat down to a simmer, with the lid on cook for another 15 minutes.

3. Add in the coconut milk, fresh basil, salt and pepper and cook for another 5 minutes.
4. After the soup has cooled a bit then puree it using an "immersion blender" **or a blender in batches.
5. Heat it through again and serve with a little Greek yogurt and garnish with a basil leaf…oh so lovely.

*Canned coconut milk can be found in any grocery store in the "Thai" food section. The "whole fat" version is what you want with no added sugars. You may need to open the can and scoop it into a bowl to whisk because the coconut fat likes to rise to the top in some brands. Coconut fat is so very good for you because it has immune-boosting properties and half of it is burned by your body for energy.

**Immersion Blender – This is an invaluable tool in the kitchen especially when it comes to partially or fully-pureeing a soup or bean stew right in the pot. Most of the immersion blenders come with an attachment so that you can puree dry ingredients as well. I've had mine for years and love it!

CARROT SOUP a la MEXICO

Yield: 8-9 cups

Spring and early summer is a most delicious time to find fresh, sweet carrots at your local farmers market and even in the grocery store. Remember to buy organic carrots and wash/scrub them well. You don't want to peel organic carrots because most of the nutrients are concentrated in and around the skin. This is why I don't care for the little "carrot nibs" for sale at the grocer with no skin and they're all the same size...what's that about? Keep in mind a farmer may use organic practices but just not have the certification from the USDA which is very labor intensive and expensive. So just ask them, "Farmer, farmer how does your garden grow?"

Ingredients:
2 tablespoons butter
2 tablespoons unrefined "virgin" coconut oil
1 medium onion, coarsely chopped
2 cloves garlic, coarsely chopped
½ teaspoon sea salt
2 pounds carrots, un-peeled, washed, ends removed
    and cut into ¼" rounds
6 cups chicken stock
1 small corn tortilla, torn into little pieces
1 ½ teaspoons ground cumin
¾ teaspoon cinnamon
2 to 2 ½ cups water to thin soup
1 ½ teaspoon sea salt and more to taste
Ground pepper
½ teaspoon cumin
¼ teaspoon cinnamon

¼ cup minced fresh cilantro
Sour cream for garnish and that little something extra!

Procedure:
1. In a 6-8 quart sauce pan over medium heat melt the butter and coconut oil and add in the onion, garlic, salt and sauté for 3-4 minutes until the onion is translucent.
2. Add in the carrots, stock, tortilla, cumin, cinnamon, bring to a boil then simmer with lid on for 35-40 minutes, until the carrots easily break apart with the back of your spoon.
3. Add in the water, salt, pepper, cumin and cinnamon again and stir well.
4. After the soup has cooled a bit then puree it using an "immersion blender"*or a regular blender in batches.
5. Heat it through again and serve with a tablespoon of sour cream and garnish with minced fresh cilantro. And, if you like a little "heat" then add a pinch of cayenne powder to your bowl.

*Immersion Blender – This is an invaluable tool in the kitchen especially when it comes to partially or fully-pureeing a soup or bean stew right in the pot. Most of the immersion blenders come with an attachment so that you can chop dry ingredients as well. I've had mine for years and love it!

5982698R0

Made in the USA
Charleston, SC
29 August 2010